Christiane Blenski

Dog Games

Stimulating play to entertain your dog and you

Hubble & Hattie

Hubble & Hattie

For more than nineteen years, the folk at Veloce have concentrated their publishing efforts on all-things automotive. Now, in a break with tradition, the company launches a new imprint for a new publishing genre!

The Hubble & Hattie imprint – so-called in memory of two, much-loved West Highland Terriers – will be the home of a range of books that cover all-things animal, produced to the same high quality of content and presentation as our motoring books, and offering the same great value for money.

More titles from Hubble & Hattie

Animal Grief: How animals mourn each other (Alderton)
Cat Speak (Rauth-Widmann)
Clever dog! Life lessons from the world's most successful animal (O'Meara)
Complete Dog Massage Manual, The – Gentle Dog Care (Robertson)
Dieting with my dog (Frezon)
Dog Cookies (Schöps)
Dog Games – stimulating play to entertain your dog and you (Blenski)
Dog Speak (Blenski)
Emergency First Aid for dogs (Bucksch)
Exercising your puppy: a gentle & natural approach – Gentle Dog Care (Robertson & Pope)
Fun and Games for Cats (Seidl)
Know Your Dog – The guide to a beautiful relationship (Birmelin)
My dog is blind – but lives life to the full! (Horsky)
My dog is deaf – but lives life to the full! (Willms)
My dog has hip dysplasia – but lives life to the full! (Haüsler)
My dog has cruciate ligament injury – but lives life to the full! (Haüsler)
Older Dog, Living with an – Gentle Dog Care (Alderton & Hall)
Smellorama – nose games for dogs (Theby)
Swim to recovery: canine hydrotherapy healing – Gentle Dog Care (Wong)
Waggy Tails & Wheelchairs (Epp)
Walkin' the dog: motorway walks for dogs & drivers (Rees)
Winston ... the dog who changed my life (Klute)
You and Your Border Terrier – The Essential Guide (Alderton)
You and Your Cockapoo – The Essential Guide (Alderton)

www.hubbleandhattie.com

Author email and website: christiane@blenski-dogs.com/www.blenski-dogs.com

Translated by Anna McLuckie

First published in February 2011 by Hubble & Hattie, Veloce House, Parkway Farm Business Park, Middle Farm Way, Poundbury, Dorchester, Dorset, DT1 3AR, England.Fax 01305 250479/e-mail info@veloce.co.uk/web www.veloce.co.uk or www.velocebooks.com.
ISBN: 978-1-845843-32-8 UPC: 6-36847-04332-2
Originally published in 2007 by Franckh-Kosmos Verlags-GmbH &Co, KG, Stuttgart, Germany.
British Library Cataloguing in Publication Data – A catalogue record for this book is available from the British Library. Typesetting, design and page make-up all by Veloce Publishing Ltd on Apple Mac.
Printed in India by Imprint Digital.

Acknowledgements

I would like to thank the dynamic team from the photo shoot, Renate Albrecht and her dog training school, Dogs in Motion, for all their brilliant support – and, of course, my dog, Jaden.

Photo credits

The photos were taken especially for the book by Sabine Stuewer (www.stuewer-tierfoto.de)/Franckh-Kosmos Verlags-GmbH & Co

Other photos

Thomas Höller: pg 22; Ulrike Schanz: pg 54; Karl-Heinz Widmann: pg 74; Karl-Heinz Widmann/Kosmos: pg 10, 11, 18, 19, 20, 21, 52, 53, 86, 110, 111

Dog Games

This is your fun wake-up call!

In the past, whether we had a puppy or an older dog, of course we all started off enthusiastically with our new companion, using knowledge gleaned from a variety of books written by excellent dog experts. We went to dog training classes at the weekend, were successful with our training, and demonstrated to our neighbours how quickly we had managed to teach sit!, down! and leave! And that was good for our dog.

However, after the first year or two, having got through canine puberty and a few other marvellous and frustrating experiences with our dog, it all simply settles down – as in all loving relationships – into everyday life. At this point nothing is new, special, or even particularly stimulating, and boredom often begins to creep in, until it's just about sweeping up dog hair in the morning and during the day, a walk in the evening, and occasionally buying a little fresh meat as a treat. You simply don't have the time for anything else; we all know how it is: children ... work ... the garden ...

You must be joking!

Of course, we all have time to throw a ball on a walk – or, instead of a ball, a Frisbee or a Kong™ which have completely different trajectories, and give the dog a different kind of work-out. And if we two-legged creatures are already out and about in the winter weather, we might also lose our gloves on the walk and then encourage our dog to look for them. We can investigate the undergrowth with him and balance along tree trunks with him, and train him to run along park benches on command. We have always got time to lay a trail of treats and create a challenging scent trail for the dog. That's right, isn't it?

Goodbye, boring routine: hello playtime!

Okay; I have to tell you: this book is not for browsing on the sofa, but has been conceived and written with the following in mind: participating, experimenting, playing, and just running around having a good time – and I mean dogs *AND* humans. It is beneficial to us two-legged creatures to live life with our dog with enthusiasm and in good spirits, and the whole family can join in – even the very smallest member. The best part of it is that every activity you do with your dog strengthens the bond between you and increases your love of and appreciation for dogs.

This book contains tried and tested game ideas and tips for activities to do with your dog. I devised all of the games, and my dog, Jaden, showed me which ones he liked best. Working together with other upbeat and energetic human-dog teams and a dog-loving photographer, I have done my best to demonstrate and explain all the games using both words and pictures. You will also find hints and tips on the subject of 'playing with your dog' in the highlighted text boxes, plus suggestions for play-related dog training in Chapter 7. There's also a test which will tell you the best game pace for you and your dog to begin with.

In this book are over 50 different dog games, waiting for you to discover them, so I won't hold you up any longer.

Have fun!

Before the games commence: a snappy warm-up

Playing? Always as a team!

Welcome to the land of laughter, because playing together makes everyone happy. In order to ensure that everybody enjoys themselves, we will abandon our role as a passive thrower of sticks, and with immediate effect! The times that your dog spent playing alone are over: now it's your turn!

At last!

As is so often the case in life, you can change things very simply by just altering your attitude. So, become your dog's playmate, game partner or team player; it doesn't matter what you call it, the crucial issue is that you are motivated to become active and involved in the games. It makes a huge difference to our dogs whether we just stand there and occasionally move our throwing arm, or run along with them, or ahead and encourage them. Our animals react enthusiastically when we adapt familiar games, go off on new paths (whether forest, field or town), and surprise them by taking part in the exercise.

"But why should I do that?" you may ask. I think you know the answer already,

1 A good mood and a real attachment are evident here: Anne and her Westie cross, Sheela, are not just dog and owner, but best friends.
2 And why? Anne says "Right from day one, I have encouraged Sheela to play, and trained her using the clicker and positive reinforcement techniques."
3 As is evident, positive reinforcement works via the stomach, too! If playing ball together can't be used as a reward, there's a tasty treat for Sheela after each success during training.

Handy tip ♡
Using a different word: cues

Here's another shift in attitude: instead of talking about 'commands,' I use the word 'cues.' This means we give the dog a verbal cue (and/or a gesture) for sit, down, etc. Imagine a set traffic lights: a green light is a signal to which we react promptly and deliberately. The training principle of positive reinforcement (more on this in Chapter 7) is based on kind and specifically unambiguous communication with your dog.

and probably have done for some time, otherwise you wouldn't be reading this book, but I'm going to tell you anyway. Playing together, doing something with your dog, trying out new ideas as a team; all are tried and tested mood-lifters. But the best reason of all is that playing together brings you closer together!

Real teamwork strengthens the bond between human and dog. I promise you, you will feel that immediately. When you are completely involved in the game, on both mental and physical levels, your dog will be more attentive for the rest of the walk – and for the rest of the day. He will react more quickly when you ask him to come or sit, and will make more eye contact with you; your motivation will allow you to really communicate with your dog and fill him with enthusiasm.

How to start, then? I have put together two options for you and test-driven them with my dog. First of all, there's the Games Guide, which contains concise explanations of all of the rules that

experience has taught me are the most important, and then there's the Game Pace Test on page 18. This leads directly to the question: is this ...

... sport or games?

Of course, I am introducing you to many ideas which require that you and your dog have a certain level of sporting ability. However, there is more to it than this: you can also play a game very quietly and calmly, at home in the living room, or out and about. There are games that require skill and still others that require focused participation from your dog. This much I know: there are small dogs, there are big dogs, young ones and old ones. And also not forgetting those that are poorly. As a responsible owner, you need to carefully select what best suits and benefits your dog. This must be your number one priority.

Games? Have the right motive!

Within the pages of this book, you will definitely find more than one game that will fully stretch your dog without putting unnecessary strain on him. If you are in any doubt about this issue, ask your vet what he or she would consider your dog's endurance limit to be. As a general rule, activity games are good for all dogs, and particularly good for animals which are recovering from an operation or an acute illness, and who are not yet completely physically fit. In these cases, clever thinking games can work absolute miracles as an alternative way to occupy and tire them.

Getting the most out of games

When you are playing with your dog, from time to time you may come across those who think your efforts are excessive; some will even tell you that you are anthropomorphising your dog, when, in fact, the opposite is the case.

When anyone says this kind of thing to me, I think of Jean Donaldson, Karen Pryor, and Gudrun Feltman, some of the dog experts who have motivated me to continue working intensively with

1a

1b

1a&b *Don't worry! Jaden and I aren't fighting; quite the opposite, in fact. I have used the cue 'pull hard!' to get him to play a tugging game. Why? I wanted to get him really interested in the flying disc, so that this toy becomes more important to him, and he will be more strongly motivated to catch it.*
2 *It's worked! Jaden chases off at top speed after his favourite orange toy, jumps up and catches it. Amazing!*
3 *He runs back to me quickly with the flying disc. This is important, because the toy, as you will soon read in the Games Guide, belongs exclusively to the human – and I want it back (only because I'm going to throw it again straight away, obviously).*
(Incidentally, if you are playing in a sandy location such as this, take at least twice as much water for your dog as you would normally.)

my dog. Their guiding principles for loving, species-appropriate handling and interaction with my dog (see Further reading on page 124) influence me on a daily basis – even when playing games.

Playmate instead of problem case

Donaldson and Feltmann emphasise the clear-cut connection between canine natural behaviour (such as hunting, searching for prey) and playing with your dog: "We are not drilling the dogs, but occupying them in order to keep these sensitive, highly specialised animals fulfilled. Dogs owned by people are not allowed – with only a few exceptions – to follow their inclination to hunt and find prey. People are excellently placed to occupy their dogs, thereby enabling them

2

Handy tip ♡

Click, clack, clicker training

The first lesson: demonstrate to your dog that every time the clicker clicks, he gets a treat. This is known as conditioning (I expect you've heard of Pavlov's dogs and the dinner bell?). Understanding this basic principle means that, for the dog, every 'click' has become a delicious confirmation that he has done something right. Clicker training is a great help with teaching new tricks, as well as a really fun way to accelerate the learning process (you can read more about this on page 116).

3

to have a good quality of life," writes Gudrun Feltmann.

Jean Donaldson voices another advantage of developing a variety of activities: "You are then not just an enlightened owner fulfilling the needs of his dog. More importantly, this type of regular stimulation is the first line of defence against behavioural problems."

Really stick with it!

Over the months when I was coping with a new baby, a young child, and working as a writer, I gradually found less and less time for Jaden and, bit-by-bit, he began to develop problematic behaviour. As soon as I became aware that I was becoming increasingly annoyed with my dog, at, for example, his excessive pulling on the lead, I made time for a short burst of clicker training with him, to play with him or to 'TTouch' him (as per the technique developed by Linda Tellington-Jones. My attention soon paid dividends. However, there are still a couple of small trouble spots which I'm working on!

My experience with Jaden was the impetus for this book. I learnt that every dog can cope for a short period of time without games, but that long-lasting neglect of this aspect of your dog's life will also result in long-lasting (negative) effects.

The games guide

1   Have you brought me something to play with, asks Nana ...?
2&3 ... and of course, Enno has!
4   Even dogs appreciate change, and each toy offers something different by way of tugging, catching, and zig-zagging all over the place. And don't forget the fun that can be had with that all-time classic – water!

The begin and end points of the game are determined by you. If your dog wants to continue after the game is over (by nudging you with his toys), ignore this completely by turning away, or leaving the room or the garden.

● Balls, Kongs™ and all other dog toys have to belong to the human, not the dog. There must be no toys lying around to which the dog can help himself. This is how he learns to pay attention to you and to play WITH you.

● Clicker training is (for me) THE key tool in activity with your dog. You can use the clicker for new games, because every click specifically tells the dog that he is doing everything right. Learning how to apply this training method is well worthwhile.

● Thirst is signalled by the dog's tongue lolling out of his mouth. But, as the way home is often a long one, and puddles at the side of the road probably won't do your dog much good, don't forget to take a bottle of fresh water and a small bowl.

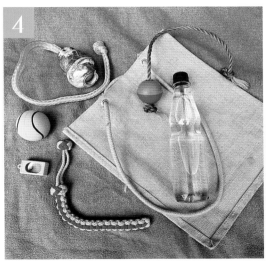

● Enthusiasm. You and your dog need plenty of this. It's important to discover which type of game or (thinking) activity is the best challenge for your dog, without overstretching him.

● Off-road – get into the woods and fields with your dog as often as possible, no matter what the conditions underfoot. You can wash off any mud later and wearing waterproof trousers and wellies will keep you dry. It's really fun to take your dog off the beaten track from time to time.

● Rabbits, deer, other animals and birds aren't just entitled to peace and protection during the nesting and breeding season. If your dog likes to disappear off hunting without your permission, find training based on positive reinforcement to remedy this.

● Keep an eye on your dog's state of health. Jumping for the ball, sudden acceleration and stopping all impact on the hips, an area where problems frequently manifest. Verify with your vet what your dog can do in terms of activity – and then do it!

● Start now – don't spend too much time thinking or talking about it. And if you have never played with your dog – or not for a while – now is the time for the human-dog team to get back into the swing of it.

● Don't use only shop-bought toys for your dog games; see what else you could use around the house. Maybe a cardboard box, an old shoe or boot. Be creative: inventing a game is fun – and free!

15

● Lead on or off? It's certainly more fun to run up hill and down dale without a lead, but not possible to do so all the time. Being on the lead doesn't mean no fun, it just means going about it differently, and you'll find lots of ideas in this book on how to do that.

● Many people feel anxious when they come across an unfamiliar dog. If a stranger approaches when you are playing, stop your game and give your dog the 'down' cue or, if he is on the lead, 'sit.' All owners have a part to play in how dogs are perceived generally, so let's all work to make sure dogs have a positive image!

● Medical treatment and operations are sometimes an unavoidable part of life. There may be times when your dog is ill and your usual routine will have to be put on hold for a while. Not to worry; you can play great games indoors, too.

Incidentally, thinking games and scent-work are particularly good for tiring out lively dogs and keeping them happy.

● 'Down,' and all the other cues are important. If you and your dog are still in need of some training, games will help in two respects: playing increases your dog's ability to focus on you, and is a fantastic reward for everything that he does right.

● Silliness. Yes, go on, just be silly with your dog from time to time. It doesn't matter what anyone else thinks, and you might even inspire someone else to have a game with their dog, so will have made another dog happy, too!

● In parks and urban areas there are often many rules for dogs and dog owners. Don't walk on the grass; keep dogs on a lead; clear up after your dog. Of course, you should observe these rules;

clear up after your dog, and keep him on the lead where required, but try not to be so restrictive that you and your dog lose sight of your mutual enjoyment.

● Use games and playing to become more confident in handling your dog. Playing will help you learn how to 'read' him better, to assess and predict his behaviour more reliably. And the more confident you feel when dealing with your dog, the more relaxed everyone around you will be in their reaction to him.

● Barter transactions help when your dog doesn't want to relinquish a toy. Try this playful offer of an exchange: when your dog has fetched ball 1, show him ball 2 and ask "Swop?" Once he has let go of ball 1, throw ball 2. You will find this works!

● Panting, barking and stopping to sniff

around can all be signs that your dog is finding the situation too much and has had enough. If he seems distracted, he is clearly signalling that he doesn't know anymore what you want from him, so stop the game. When you resume later, break down the teaching into smaller increments.

● Be clear and consistent. You ask for the ball, but your dog brings the stick? Insist on the ball. This is how you challenge your dog intellectually. And anyone who thinks his dog is stupid will soon be convinced otherwise – I'm convinced of that!

● How sure are you that you dog will do as you ask? "He'll probably bring the ball ... he'll probably come back." If your dog 'switches off' from you, redouble your concentration on him and remain full of surprises. There are endless opportunities in this respect – use one on every walk.

● Does your dog like to get into arguments with other dogs? My favourite tip may help here: a tired dog is a good dog, so decide on a cue word – Yes! Yo! Go! – that encourages your dog to keep on searching, keep on running, keep on playing. And for those dogs which need

to have their enthusiasm for play (re-) awakened, work on your best inspirational and motivational voice.

● Tugging games are allowed: they do not encourage your dog to be aggressive; completely the opposite, in fact. A tugging game is ideal for demonstrating the difference between the desired behaviours of pulling, tugging, and biting down, and the cue 'give!' But only use this when you are comfortable with it.

The big game pace test: part 1

Meetings, time and wet weather

Please answer all questions by choosing the statement which best suits you and your dog

Question 1
Recently, my dog has been really ...
- a Impetuous and very keen to be on the go
- b Interested in playing with other dogs, but not with me
- c Prefers his toys to other dogs
- d Tired, listless and physically weak – he doesn't even eat treats
- e Inconsistent, different every day. I don't know where I am with him
- f   Quickly becomes aggressive, barks a lot, doesn't listen to me
- g In good form, consistent, a great partner

Question 2
It's raining cats and dogs. If you are completely honest, you would prefer to ...
- a Run out quickly with the dog and then run just as quickly back home
- b Wait until the rain eases off a bit and then take your usual walk
- c Put the dog out in the garden on his own, and resolve to take him for a longer-than-usual walk tomorrow

Question 3

If you were to put down this book now and talk to your dog, what is it that he actually reacts to?

- ○ a Movement. When I stand up from the sofa, he comes to my side immediately
- ○ b When I call his name or tempt him with a ball. Otherwise, he remains lying down
- ○ c It's difficult to motivate my dog. *He* decides when he feels like getting up and coming to me

Question 4

When we meet other people and dogs, I ...

- ○ a Remove the lead immediately so that my dog can go and say hello to his friends
- ○ b Turn on my heel and beat a retreat, or ensure that we pass the others quickly
- ○ c Quickly put the lead on and wait to see how the other dog(s) react. If they're okay, then I'm fine with the dogs playing together
- ○ d Nothing, because my dog isn't interested in other dogs or other people
- ○ e We simply continue on

Question 5

Work, children, housework, garden: there's always so much to do. Think back over the last three days and add up the time you have consciously chosen to spend with your dog

- ○ a In all honesty, not more than 3 hours
- ○ b Between 6 and 7 hours, I think
- ○ c Definitely more than 10 hours
- ○ d Much more than that – I choose to be with my dog 24 hours a day

Now, carry on to part 2

The big game pace test: part 2

Dreams, emotions, feelings

Please answer all questions by choosing the statement which best applies to you and your dog

Question 6
Imagine a situation in which you and your dog are getting on really well. What would you be doing?
- ○ a Cuddling – we are snuggled up together
- ○ b Playing – we are happily engaged in exercise
- ○ c Competition – we are doing an agility course together
- ○ d Children – the whole family is romping with the dog in the garden

Question 7
Life with your dog undoubtedly has its highs and lows. How does it seem to be at the moment?
- ○ a My dog and I are a really good team and are looking for new challenges
- ○ b My dog and I haven't quite got the hang of working together, so I want to do some more work with him
- ○ c We're in a 'low' at the moment, frustrated and not having fun together any more
- ○ d A bit mixed. It's obvious that the more I do with my dog, the better we get on, but as soon as I spend less time on him, there are problems

Question 8
Margriet Eshuijs sings, "Sometimes I wish I was my dog." What do you envy/admire about your dog?
- ○ a He is so fast and fit, and has such good stamina – I wish I was as fit and chipper

b   My dog is always happy. I would like to be as positive as he is

c   Not to have to do anything – just eat, sleep and be stroked. His life seems
    amazingly relaxed

d   A dog is a dog. A human is a human. What's to envy or admire?

Question 9

When you are interacting with your dog, you are usually ...

a   in the house, flat or garden

b   in the park

c   outside and on the go – even with the bike

d   always somewhere different

Interested to see how you've done? Turn to page 24 and use the table to work out your
score. In the meantime, and by way of relaxation after your hard work, there follows a
humorous story on the subject of all-weather fun for dogs ...

My dog's job ...

Keno the weatherman

No matter what the weather is like, my dog is delighted with it. I am amazed to hear of dogs who, when it's raining, run on tiptoes through wet grass and want to be dried off immediately after paddling or swimming in a stream. Other examples of animals who are the opposite of Keno are those that want only to lie in the cool hallway when it's hot, or feel miserable if there is any wind, hail or snow. There is no type of weather that can spoil Keno's fun when he goes for a walk. Even in a really hot summer, instead of taking it slowly he will race tirelessly from one shady spot to the next, where he will lie briefly, slurp a little water to perk himself up, and then quickly scout for the next bush with a patch of shady ground.

You might think that he doesn't actually care about the weather, but that's not it at all. Managing every weather situation is a daily task and challenge that he takes very seriously, because his attitude is that all weather, no matter what kind, should be utilised as an especially pleasurable canine experience. And this is how that approach works: when rain has made the ground nice and soft, Keno enthusiastically slides around in the slushy and fairly sticky mud. If we have some snowy winter weather, Keno rushes into the snow, using his muzzle as a snowplough, and his nose as a snorkel, rushing wildly backwards and forwards across the beautifully iced landscape. In gale force winds, Keno seeks out the highest points outside, such as heaps of sand or dunghills, and stands on the top, all four paws braced in order to let the wind really blow through his coat.

This determination to go out in every sort of weather means that even if we lived in a windowless flat, we would know exactly what kind of weather there was at any given time, thanks to how Keno's coat is. He is, therefore, our weatherman who, in order to determine the weather, requires only a short trip into the garden for a sniff and a wee, with no necessity for any special meteorological equipment. Upon his return, just one look at his coat will tell you exactly what that day's weather is like.

For instance, light green grass stains on his paws mean it is dry and mild. Wet patches on the carpet can be traced back to ice balls on his paws, which in turn point to there being snow on the ground; at least 10cm of it. The sound of sandy soil slowly dropping and scattering on the laminate flooring means light rain, with only slightly damp ground. Large clumps of dirt falling onto the floor mean the weather is horrible. Slightly frizzy fur on the neck, ears and tail is the result of swirls of early morning fog.

Incidentally, the only old wives' tale about the weather that you can confidently completely ignore in Keno's case is "If a dog is eating grass, it's going to rain soon," because he eats almost as much grass as a cow, and his grass-eating habits have definitely never had any influence on the weather.

But what I really love about Keno – whatever the weather – is the powerful, cyclone-like shaking that he performs in the hallway straight after his walk. I can tell what the weather is like from the state of the wallpaper (which used to be white, incidentally). I have tried to clicker train this shaking. However, even when I use the cue word 'shake!' outside the front door, he has another ferocious shake when two or three steps inside the door, and of course always on those days when I don't think he's going to!

This weather association may well be something to do with the 'bolt of lightning' that hit us the first time we saw Keno, when, as a sweet little puppy, he 'stormed' into our hearts. After all, when there's a strong spark like that, it must be love – regardless of the weather!

Add up the points to determine your score. And remember, what really counts here is fun!

Question 1
a 8 points   b 5 points   c 4 points   d 1 point   e 3 points   f 2 points
g 6 points

Question 2
a 4 points   b 6 points   c 2 points

Question 3
a 8 points   b 4 points   c 2 points

Question 4
a 6 points   b 2 points   c 4 points   d 3 points   e 8 points

Question 5
a 2 points   b 3 points   c 4 points   d 6 points

Question 6
a 2 points   b 4 points   c 8 points   d 6 points

Question 7
a 8 points   b 4 points   c 2 points   d 6 points

Question 8
a 8 points   b 4 points   c 3 points   d 1 point

Question 9
a 2 points   b 4 points   c 6 points   d 8 points

16 to 25 points
'ARMCHAIR ATHLETE'

ASSESSMENT: You and your dog like a quiet life, and your dog is not very fit, either for reasons of health or age. No matter, you can both have some fun, because it's still possible to play, even in the living room. Take it in small steps. If your dog simply doesn't want to play (with you!), you'll find some helpful hints in the next few pages.

STARTING GAME PACE: Chapter 3; eg 'Taking it lying down.'

MOTIVATION: Acknowledge your dog's consistency and inner calm with pride – and his watchful intelligence. But remember that he still wants to be occupied, and amused and entertained.

26 to 39 points
'WHERE'S THE SPARK?'

ASSESSMENT: Yes, you make the time – for long walks. You and your dog are also very happy, but, if you're honest, there are issues with training and with team spirit. Everything could be better, but somehow there is never enough time, and you ask yourself how do you occupy a dog, anyway? Isn't it a bit silly, playing with your dog? No! It's extremely worthwhile, is the answer to that. So, begin the journey ... the objective? Quite obviously: use play and games to reawaken your dog's enthusiasm for you – and yours for him!

STARTING GAME PACE: Chapter 4; eg 'Which one's the ball?'

MOTIVATION: Your dog can run and run and run. He has incredible hearing, a fantastically good nose, and excellent sight. He doesn't have all of this just so that he can spend his time lying in his basket. Start slowly, but start today!

40 to 59 points
'EXPERIENCED PACESETTER'

ASSESSMENT: Oh yes, your dog is really on the ball – and so are you – but every time you want to get enthusiastically involved with your dog, there's always something else – children, friends, family – demanding attention during what little free time you have. Well, just get them all to play together with you! Or consider how you can up the pace of what little playtime you have. Your dog is capable of a great deal: use it!

STARTING GAME PACE: Chapter 4; eg 'Human obstacle course.'

MOTIVATION: Now's the best time to increase your dog's selection of toys. Don't just stick with a ball, and don't just play alone. You know that good moods are infectious!

60 points and over
'PERFORMANCE ACCELERATOR'

ASSESSMENT: Stop, stop, stop! Yes, it's obvious that your dog is an all-rounder, an athlete who enjoys both brain-work and scent-work. But now it's time to raise the bar – not in terms of objective, but in quality of performance. This demands more from your dog than standard athleticism; it requires thinking, concentration, skill and fitness, a combination of abilities that will set a completely different kind of pace for your dog.

STARTING GAME PACE: Chapter 5; eg 'Don't lose your bottle!'

MOTIVATION: You are an extremely active 'dog person:' well done! Now you can find out again what delights your dog. Not through being ambitious, but by being creative. Incredibly rewarding!

Playing – without my dog

"Not interested!" This is what you imagine your dog is thinking when you wave a ball in front of him. You've always known this; your dog simply does not want to play. And that's a great shame as playing games together fosters team spirit between human and dog. So don't give up, as even *your* dog has the ability to jump, chase, tug, search, catch, sniff and sprint, you just have to awaken these dormant abilities. In a lecture, dog expert and wolf researcher Erik Ziemen described our four-legged friends as "... young wolves, who never grow up." Essentially, this means that they retain forever a youthful state of mind, and play is very much a part of this.

From nought to fun in 6 steps

● Presentation. Show your dog a toy (a ball, say) by playing with it yourself. Throw it up high, roll it or bounce it, make a big performance out of your game, but be sure not to include your dog. After a few such performances, your dog will show some interest when you next produce the toy.

● Quick tip. Has your dog become inattentive? Then offer the toy to your dog for only a short time. Perhaps throw the ball a little way and run after it yourself, encouraging the dog to do the same. Does your dog join in? Progress! Be pleased and stop the game! Why? Because it is important to end the game before your dog loses interest.

● Surprise! Keep producing the toy over a period of days and weeks – sometimes in the morning, sometimes on your walk, sometimes in the house. It appears, you play for a short time, it disappears again. If your dog's enthusiasm is increasing, you are already halfway there.

● The power of imagination. After your next attempt at playing, sit down quietly and close your eyes. Imagine your dog

1   French Mastiffs are great guys. They set their own pace and know their own mind. Playing? They often have no time for that kind of frivolity
2&3 With her dedicated efforts, Tanja manages to get her young dog, Campino, interested in the toy
4   Job done with a quick tugging game. They're off the starting blocks!

4

playing with a toy (and with you!). What form does the play take? Does your dog run after the Kong™ or does he catch a ball? Whatever occurs to you first and whatever pleases you even when you just think about it, do that – and only that – for your first game!

● Slice-by-slice. Divide the game that you have visualised into sections. For example, your dog runs after the ball, picks it up, brings it back and gives it to you. Practice each section on its own and begin with the section of the game about which your dog is the most enthusiastic. Use this method to put the game together, section by section. When training your dog to play, never forget to be actively involved in the game and praise enthusiastically.

● Build on your successes. Have you managed to get your dog to play with you?

Well done! Now bring new elements into the game, such as other toys, or variations on the game. This ensures that your dog will remain a dedicated game player and should never become bored.

Handy tip ♡

The prey instinct

Every dog – including yours! – has the hunting instinct, which you can use to help motivate play. A ball on a rope is particularly well suited to this, because you can pull it along the ground and zigzag it backwards and forwards. A dog will love running after his 'prey,' but don't move the toy towards him; instead, move it it quickly away from him.

Before the games commence: check

- √ You determine the beginning and end of the game
- √ Keep varying the games and trying out new ones
- √ Vary the type of challenge between brain-work, skill and pace
- √ Don't always buy new toys - make creative use of what you have at home
- √ Stop before your dog loses interest
- √ Tailor the type of game to the ability, age and health status of your dog
- √ Actively play with your dog and don't forget to show enthusiasm!

On your marks, get set, let's go – your first games & your first successes

So, how do we play this?

Games for beginners

Small but surprising!

I'm right at home here!
46

On your marks, get set:
check
48

Get well soon!
42

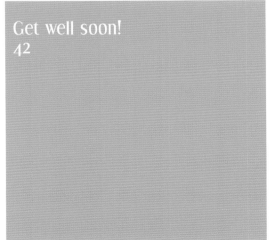

So, how do we play this?

You know the rules of play, you've done enough reading, and you just want to get on with the games ... Well, I don't want to hold you back; on the contrary! After all, this book is intended to be an ideas store, waiting to be used by you.

My explanations of the different games are concise, and always use the same keywords. The explanation is accompanied by one or more photos which explain the aim of the game, and there's also an assessment of the game's level of difficulty (from ♡ for beginners to ♡♡♡♡ for experts). A list of 'fun ingredients' tells you what you need for the particular game. The section *Variations on this theme* suggests different ways of playing the game. Once you get practicing and playing you will certainly be able to add some of your own.

I would like to motivate you

Yes, I would like to motivate you to not only don your reading glasses, but also to pick up a pen. Use the book as your personal notebook: mark games that you want to try out with your dog; use different colours, for example, green for the games that you want to start with, red for the ones you think will be challenging, and blue for those that you can already do. Make a note of the date when you first try out a game and write down your dog's reaction. If you are lucky enough to have several dogs, you can also record which

1 Sam the Golden Retriever is stressed. Birthe wants him to hold the piece of rope in his mouth for a photo. She says 'sit!' and 'hold!'
2 But Sam doesn't cooperate. He has had his photo taken for this book many times already today, and has had enough of his unaccustomed star status. He stands up and swerves away from Birthe.
3&4 Sam jumps up. He would rather do anything than sit still. He needs a break from concentrating. Birthe recognises this and plays with him for a short while.
5 Now Sam has calmed down again and looks expectantly at Birthe. His attitude says: "I am ready."

dog tried out the game with you. I have noticed that it can be really motivating if you set yourself goals and then achieve them; noting your progress so that you can look back over what you and your dog have accomplished together as a team.

Warning: stress!

"My dog barks the whole time!"
"Mine begins to pant very quickly."
It may be that your dog is thirsty. However, it may also be the case that your dog is stressed? Stressed by play? Yes, our division of time into serious work and fun playtime is incomprehensible to dogs, because we also expect certain behaviour from our dog when we play with him. Whether he is catching the ball or placing his backside on the ground in response to the 'sit' cue, in each case he has to fulfil our expectations and concentrate.

So it's important to notice when displacement activities – such as barking, yowling, panting, tongue flickering (constant licking of the nose), yawning, sniffing and becoming either very slow or hyperactive – are signs of stress. Nothing works when a dog is stressed, so if this is the case, stop the exercise immediately and play a game with your dog that he knows inside out. Then praise him extravagantly and have a well-earned break.

A little assignment
Note down the answers to the following questions –

● Why do you want to play (more) with your dog?
● What are your expectations? Be aware of your motivation and your goals. After all, you had a reason for buying this book, didn't you?
● Why are you putting so much thought into this? (Because it's worth it!)

When all is said and done, any partnership with an amazing companion such as a dog has its highs and its lows, and I sincerely hope that you share my experience of continuously rediscovering why I love my dog so much. Because what actor Heinz Rühmann said is completely true: "Obviously, you *can* live without a dog, but it's just not worth it."

33

Games for beginners

The washing thief
Level of difficulty: ♡ to ♡♡♡
You will need: socks, clothes pegs,
treats, washing line, 1 dog, 2 people

How to do it

From now on, don't throw away old socks; keep them for this game!

Hang three or four clean socks on a washing line with pegs, as shown in the pictures (height is obviously dependent on the size of your dog). Hide a treat in each sock as an incentive for your dog to firstly sniff at it and then tug hard enough to pull it off the line. Really cheer him on whilst he's doing this to boost his confidence. If your dog is frightened or alarmed by the clothes peg falling or pinging off, simply hang the socks over the washing line without pegs. In order to make the game a little more interesting, you can hold the line at an angle so that some of the socks are more difficult to reach.

Variations on this theme

A really easy version of this is to just attach treats – chewy strips, say – to the

Washing thief

1   Katy and Nick hold the washing line just high enough so that their chirpy Parson Russell Buddy can reach the socks ...
2   ... but has to exert himself to do so. A game for dogs of any age; children also enjoy participating and holding the washing line.

umbrella-jump, give him lots of praise. He may not get the idea straight away, though, so here are a couple of tips:

1   At first, simply place the umbrella on the ground and allow your dog to walk or run over it, so that he understands the principle.

2   Limit his opportunities for avoidance by holding the umbrella against a fence or wall on one side.

Jolly brolly

1   *Buddy joyously jumps over the umbrella. This is a game he knows and loves. If your dog still needs guidance for this jump into playtime happiness, take an umbrella with you on walks, even on sunny days, and practice when you are out and about. It will make a nice change of pace for your dog!*

line, which will introduce your dog to the game in a very tasty way. The degree of difficulty can be increased by not allowing your dog to just drop the sock after he has pulled it off the line, but ask that he bring it to you or place it in a basket.

Jolly brolly
Level of difficulty: ♡ to ♡ ♡
You will need: 1 umbrella, 1 dog,
1 person

How to do it
Cue your dog to sit, then, at a distance of approximately twice your dog's body length away from him, hold out the furled umbrella horizontally. With your other hand, throw a ball (or treats) over the umbrella, at the same time giving your dog the cue for 'go!' or 'fetch the ball!' If your dog takes the direct route over the

Variations on this theme

Change the height of the jump, depending on the size and ability of your dog. You can also open the umbrella, rest it on the ground and have your dog look for something behind it (hold the umbrella still so that it doesn't move and scare/injure your dog). And another idea: hold the furled umbrella in a verticle position and ask your dog to circle it following a treat. This is easier to do with two people – one to hold the umbrella and one to do the enticing with a treat. After two or three trials using a treat, encourage your dog to do it without a tasty inducement, and link the circling with a new cue, such as 'round!' Your dog will soon be able to circle on command. If you can lay your hands on several umbrellas, turn to page 63 and move straight on to the umbrella slalom!

Yoghurt pot memory game
Level of difficulty: ♡ to ♡♡
You will need: Lots of the same type of clean yoghurt pots, treats, 1 pen, 1 dog, 1 person

How to do it

So, does your family like yoghurt? That's good! From now on, collect the empty pots – as many of the same type as possible – and wash them out well. Mark two of these pots with a pen. With your dog sitting, put two treats in front of him and place the marked pots upside-down over the top of them. Give the cue 'go!' or 'search!' and see if your dog can retrieve the treats from under the pots. After repeating this a few times, increase the level of difficulty so that it becomes a memory test. Cover the treats with

the two marked pots and then place as many other similar pots around them as possible. This is when it gets interesting: how does he go about finding the treats? Did he make a mental note of the two pots, perhaps, or simply use his nose to check out all of the pots before eventually finding the treats? Don't forget to give him encouragement!

Variations on this theme
You can make this even more difficult by having your dog wait in another room whilst you set up the yoghurt pots. You can also make this a fun game for children if you stack several yoghurt pots into a structure resembling a house of cards, and hide the pots with the treats in the midst of these.

Essentially, this is a scenting game – yoghurt pots are no good at all as chew toys, so preclude any attempt to bite the pots with a sharply expressed cue such as 'no!'

Star ball
Level of difficulty: ♡ to ♡ ♡
You will need: 3 balls, 1 person, 1 dog

How to do it
Does your dog love chasing balls? Does

he also give them back to you when you are playing? He will in this game, because in your hand you will have three balls that your dog can pick up quickly and easily. Squat in the middle of the lawn, field or path, and call your dog to you. Then throw the balls one at a time, ensuring that your dog returns the one just thrown before you throw the next. Don't throw the balls in the same direction, but in different directions every time, which will keep him on his toes as he will not know which way the balls will go!

Variations on this theme
Of course, you can do practically anything with a ball. Instead of throwing or rolling the balls, stand up and bounce them away from you so that your dog has to follow their trajectory. Instead of a ball, why not use a Kong™, or another type of toy for this game?

37

Small but surprising!

Tasty treat tube
Level of difficulty ♡ to ♡♡
You will need: 1 cardboard tube from the inside of a toilet roll or a roll of kitchen paper, treats, 1 dog, 1 person

How to do it

Small dogs are good with their noses; as many toys are much too big for them, they use their noses to push them along. This game is all about the correct method of propulsion.

Put some treats into the tube, and then stuff both ends with kitchen paper so that the treats don't fall out during the game. Place the tube in front of your dog and encourage him as soon as he touches the tube with his nose and makes it roll. Once your dog has understood that this game is about using his nose to push the tube, ask him to sit, place the tube in front of him and walk two or three paces away. Now encourage your dog to roll the tube to you. Once he has done this, take out the kitchen paper and give him the treats.

Variations on this theme

The game can be made more difficult by

1

Tasty treat tube

1   *Beagles are scent workers. Anabel pushes the cardboard tube excitedly across the grass.*
2   *And now she's allowed to get the treat out.*
3   *Success! She's done it.*

Creepy-crawly

1   *Renate squats in the grass in front of Clara with a treat in her hand, which is lying on the ground. When Renate pulls her hand away, Clara crawls after it.*

increasing the distance between you and your dog, so that he has further to push the tube before receiving his treats. Vary the game by using a large ball or even a balloon instead of the treat-filled tube. The completely different weights – and the fact that the ballon floats rather than rolls – makes this a new challenge for your dog.

Creepy-crawly

Level of difficulty: ♡ to ♡ ♡
You will need: 1 dog, 1 person, lots of treats, a favourite toy

How to do it

Give your dog the 'down' cue and squat in front of him. Under your cupped hand on the ground you have a few, very strong-smelling treats: hold this hand right in front of your dog's nose. If your dog stretches his neck and touches your hand, give him one of the treats. Move back a little: the aim is to get your dog to creep after the hand that has the treats. If your dog stands up, immediately tell him 'down!and start again. If he now crawls forward across the ground, praise him enthusiastically. After three or four practice attempts, let him stand up and run around.

Variations on this theme
You can vary this game by getting your dog to creep through something (see 'Tunnel runner' on thist page), or can develop the idea into a 'rollover.' This means getting your dog – from the starting position of lying on his front – to roll on his back from one side to the other. When you are practicing, first reward him when he lies on his side. Take a treat and, holding it just above his head, move it from one side to the other, so that he has to roll over in order to follow it. With some dogs, this works straightaway, but others need more practice before getting it right.

Tunnel runner
Level of difficulty ♡♡
You will need: 1 cardboard box, 1 dog, 1 person

How to do it
Make a narrow tunnel out of a cardboard box by folding in or cutting off the top

and bottom. Roll a treat or a favourite ball into or through the tunnel; does your dog react with interest and run after it?

Great! Reward him. If your dog is not keen on going through the tunnel, reward him as soon as he puts his head inside it and for every step he takes into it. Or hold a particularly tasty treat the other side of the tunnel.

Once your dog has understood what he is supposed to do, you can build a course of tunnels – differently sized if you wish – in your living room or in the garden. Or vary the angle of the tunnel with a broad plank or board; every variation represents a new challenge for your dog.

Variations on this theme
Be more involved in the game and actually become a tunnel for your dog by getting down on all fours so that your dog can run

Get down to his level!

Try seeing the world from the point of view of your Dachshund, Westie or Pug: how high everything is, how threatening even the smallest child can seem. All dogs, but small dogs in particular, have a problem with people leaning over them. For this reason, it is important that when you are playing with, stroking, or grooming your dog, you remember to squat down beside rather than lean over him. Games such as the 'Tunnel runner' also help your dog to become braver, more self-confident, and free from fear in his everyday life.

underneath you, between your arms and your legs. This is another game in which children will undoubtedly want to be involved. Brilliant!

The sock seeker
Level of difficulty: ♡
You will need: 1 small material bag (or a sock), 1 person, 1 dog, treats

How to do it
Give your dog a bag (or sock) filled with five or six treats to sniff, then tell him 'down!' Hide the bag in another room (or somewhere in the garden, or in a bush if you are out for a walk). Now go back to him and give him the cue for 'seek!' Once your dog has found the treat bag treasure, reward him with a treat from it. Again, give the cue 'down!' and hide the bag somewhere else, continuing in this way until the bag is empty.

Variations on this theme
Hide the treat-filled sock amongst a pile of other socks, the bag in a pile of old (dog) towels, or perhaps under a pile of leaves if outside. This requires the dog to use his scenting abilities and also to do a little rummaging. As, before, repeat until the bag or sock is empty.

Get well soon!

Towel touch

1-4 Initially, Sam only looks through the hole, but eventually becomes brave enough to take the first step. By only his second attempt he is happily jumping through.

Towel touch
Level of difficulty: ♡♡
You will need: 1 old bed sheet or towel,
1 pair of scissors, 1 dog, 1 or 2 people

How to do it
If your dog is recovering from an illness
or operation, he may not be able to move
around as much as usual, but that doesn't
mean he should lie about all day, either.
Use some of his recuperation time to
improve body awareness.

Make two cuts in the shape of a cross
in the middle of an old bed sheet, so that
the hole is just large enough for your dog
to pass through. Then familiarise your dog
with the sheet and show him the opening.
Use treats or his favourite chewy bone to
encourage him bit by bit through the hole.
Once your dog has understood that he is
supposed to step through the hole in the
sheet, stretch the sheet between you and
a helper so that your dog can step through
very elegantly all by himself. This works
on the same principle as the use of body
bands or massage techniques such as
TTouch created by Linda Tellington-Jones
(see Further reading in Chapter 8), and
means that when your dog slips through
the sheet, he experiences a completely
new way of being aware of his body, which
will give him a positive feeling from his
head to his tail.

Variations on this theme
You can combine stepping through a sheet
with another game by setting up the sheet
at the end of a tunnel, for example. And
you can repeatedly surprise your dog by
always having something different behind
the cloth: a special bone, perhaps. I am
sure you can come up with any number of
ideas for surprises!

Taking it lying down
Level of difficulty: ♡
You will need: 1 dog, 1 or two people

How to do it
The game is simple and also simply
brilliant. You and your partner or your
children lie down on the ground. Each
person hides treats about their body: in
a hand, in the turn-ups of trousers, or
in the top of a sock. Your dog must wait
until you give the 'seek!' command, and
then he can get sniffing, calmly, using his
instincts. This game doesn't just fulfil the

Taking it lying down

1-3 Birthe hides the treat in her trouser turn-up. Will Sam find it? He keeps on sniffing until he does.

43

objective of entertaining a poorly dog, it also strengthens the bond between you and your dog through close contact.

Variations on this theme
Hide something underneath your body so that your dog has to ask you to move, perhaps by gently nudging you with his nose. To introduce the idea initially, simply hide a toy such as a ball or a chewy toy under your knees when you are sitting down. Keep in mind, though, that your dog will usually only enjoy playing a game if he quickly has some experience of success.

Catch my eye!
Level of difficulty: ♡
You will need: 1 dog, 1 person, 1 toy or several treats

How to do it
This very quiet, calm game helps your dog to recuperate and also improves communication between you. It's very simple, but extremely effective – and this is how it works.

Every time your dog makes unsolicited eye contact with you, reward him with praise, a treat, or a short (calm!) game.

Don't call him, but just keep a close eye on him. Begin by rewarding every glance in your direction, so that, as soon as he looks at you, something nice happens. Later on, only reward him when he looks directly at your face. Do not, however, on any account reward your dog's (longing) glances at the treats, otherwise he will not focus on anything else.

Variations on this theme
Does your dog know his name? Are you sure? It's often, in fact, not the case with young dogs. Call your dog by his name and, when he responds, throw him a treat

or praise him warmly and briefly. Keep calling him at random points throughout the day. However, keep the eye-catching game and the name-calling game completely separate from each other, and practice on different days to prevent confusion.

Catch my eye!

1&2 This is what a team looks like: Sam maintains eye contact with Birthe. Of course, he noticed long ago that she has a treat hidden behind her back, but he will only get this after he has held her gaze for a while.

Ball fishing
Level of difficulty: ♡ to ♡♡
You will need: a ball or Kong™ on a cord, 1 person, 1 dog

How to do it
Is your dog allowed to walk or run, but not jump? If so, this game is ideal because instead of throwing the ball, which would entail him running, turning sharply and sometimes jumping, you simply hold out the ball and your dog can 'fish' for it.

Ask your dog to 'sit (or 'stand') and then position yourself two or three metres away with your legs wide apart. Dangle a ball or Kong™ on a cord behind you. Ask your dog to 'fetch the ball!' If your dog is unwell, it is, of course, important that you stay very calm, and do not excite him in any way with your voice. Look behind you so that you can monitor his pace.

Variations on this theme
It's fun to play this game from time to time on walks, just dangling the ball behind you so that your dog can fish for it. Once

Ball fishing

1-3 Campino wants the ball, so walks unhurriedly through Tanja's straddled legs and grabs the cord.

your dog is fit again, you can hold the ball up high so that he has to jump up to get it. Or wedge it into a bush or the cleft of a branch so that only the rope is hanging down. Your dog has first to search for the ball and then fish for it. One of my favourite games when we are out for a walk!

I'm right at home here!

Spic and span
Level of difficulty: ♥♥ to ♥♥♥
You will need: 1 towel, 1 person, 1 dog

How to do it

A clean house – thanks to your dog? It can be from now on with this game! Place a towel on the ground in front of your dog. Every time he approaches the towel and puts his paw on it, reward him. The aim is to get your dog pushing the towel backwards and forwards with his front paws, so specifically praise movements in the right direction. The key here is to reward at exactly the right point: even if he moves the towel only slightly with his paws say "Wipe!" every time, so that he links the word with his action. After a few days' practice, he will be able to clean the floor really well. Very useful on days when he has dirty paws!

Variations on this theme

Does your dog trust you? Do the towel test. Ask your dog to lie down on the towel and begin to pull the towel – slowly at first and then more rapidly through the room or along the hallway. If your dog does not jump off, he trusts you, and is also brave. If he runs away, try again, pulling very cautiously and gently at first. You will see how his trust increases day by day.

Spic and span

1-3 Jaden is an expert at this. First, paws on the towel, then move the paws on the towel, and wipe away!
4 Absolute trust: Jaden lets me pull him along on the towel.

Stair climber
Level of difficulty: ♡ to ♡♡
You will need: 1 person, 1 dog, lots of treats

How to do it

If your dog is familiar with the 'sit' cue, he can play this game. The objective is to 'slow down' your dog when he's in the house – and to be very calm yourself when playing the game. You need a handful of small treats and some stairs. Climb the stairs with your dog, but don't hurry; go up one step at a time. So far, so good. Back down at the bottom, mount one step and then cue your dog to sit. Once he's done this, climb up onto the next step; wait, and then call him up as well. Again, ask him to sit, climb the next step, call him, etc, until you have reached the top. A day or two later repeat this combination of calm-training-concentration, but not on every step. Do it every two steps, then every four steps, and the next time you do it, stop only on one step. This exercise forces your dog to concentrate on you 100 per cent of the time – and in a completely calm and quiet way.

Variations on this theme

You can also do this exercise outdoors. When walking, suddenly stop and look around you, completely ignoring your four-legged friend until he comes and sits down beside you. Praise him and carry on walking. Your dog should not be able to predict when you stop – sometimes stop after just a couple of steps and sometimes not until you get round the next corner. This a lovely, simple way of keeping your dog's attention.

Stair climber

1-3 A great deal of concentration is required to play this game outside, but this special 'finale' is great for letting off steam. Have your dog on a lead and ask him to sit. unclip the lead and run ahead. He must wait until you call him before running to join you.

on your marks, get set, let's go: check

√ Use what you have at home for the games

√ Check your choices of toy for any hidden dangers

√ Take time to familiarise your dog with new objects

√ When something works, praise your dog
   enthusiastically; if something goes wrong, simply ignore
   it and try again later

√ Sometimes play outside, sometimes inside, and
   sometimes with an audience - new situations are
   challenging for your dog (and you!)

√ Once you have succeeded with a game, vary it to keep
   it fresh and exciting

Something for the sports stars

Sporty dog!
52

My dog's job ...
The timekeeper
54

Leads off!
56

Lead on!
60

Something for the
sports stars: check
68

Get fitter!
62

Very clever!
66

51

Sporty dog!

If you are really happy to keep up a smart pace when out and about with your four-legged friend, whether you are covering long distances on foot, jogging or walking briskly, or even going really fast on a bike, I don't want to stop you from doing this. Keep on going – but be circumspect.

In the book *Teach your dog to think* by Nina Miodragovic, I found two important tips to sporting activity with dogs. However, I don't make any firm distinction between playing together and training together. Of course, doing athletic activities with your dog requires exact and committed work from you both, and is recommended for every athletic dog that is keen to learn. All the same, actively playing together is also an intensive preliminary stage of training, and you can be equally proud of all your successes in this respect. According to Miodragovic (and others), two things need to be borne in mind: "Jogging and cycling should be done in moderation. We aren't aiming for high performance athletes, just dogs with reasonable stamina." Secondly, she makes it clear that having a break from time to time is part of learning. She writes: "In order for the brain to consolidate the desired and recently linked connections, it is of utmost importance that the dog spends some time after the learning period in a low stimulation environment that is as stress-free as possible. The best thing he can do is go to sleep."

A period of calm is therefore crucial after a demanding game, and enables our dogs to get their heads together for the next training session. (You will discover

1&2 Which of the two of us is more athletic? My dog is certainly faster – so jogging with me doesn't tire him at all. We need a game!
3&4 Before you begin playing, ensure your dog's muscles are warmed up!
5   You really need to practice cycling with your dog. Always bear in mind that he should be running in a relaxed manner alongside the bike; if he is frightened or wary of it, don't force him to do this.

5

Handy tip ♡

Everyday fitness!

Quickening your usual pace will get you and your dog physically fit, and your everyday life will also be more relaxed. Why? Well, when dogs develop undesirable behaviours, it is generally because they are bored and under-stimulated, both physically and mentally, so games which are challenging are good for canine wellbeing. Physical exercise and experience of success enable your dog to become a well-balanced, alert and obedient companion for life. Don't miss this opportunity of getting fit together!

in Chapter 7, A break in play, how your dog learns and how to use positive reinforcement to make the most of all the work you do with him.)

As soon as we leave the house, my dog is not interested in peace and quiet. He tends to over-exert himself, and runs until his tongue is virtually dragging on the ground. But he still manages to mobilize himself constantly to chase after the ball. In fact, about two metres into our walk, he would be happy to run straight to our 'games field' and tear off after a flying disc immediately. We don't do this, of course, because every dog needs to warm up before exercise; it's also important not to underestimate the importance of a cooling off and warming down period after the game, or after cycling or jogging.

But I expect you are aware of this and are already doing the right thing, and now you and your speedy four-legged friend are ready for some new ideas and a new impetus.

Before you start, however, I would like to offer you the chance to read another of my personal experiences with Keno. It dovetails perfectly with the extra tip on this page ...

You make the decisions!

In the middle of a game, you stop to find a handkerchief to blow your nose. Your dog barks; you look up and quickly throw the ball. This is a situation where your dog acted and you reacted. It should be the other way round: you cue 'sit!' and your dog does so. You find and use your hankie, then cue the release from 'sit' and throw the ball.

These little things reinforce the idea that we humans are the managers, and our dogs can focus and rely on us. So be proactive in maintaining control and being reliable for your dog.

My dog's job ...

The timekeeper

"Your dog's got a screw loose," my mother frequently tells me, shaking her head. But completely the opposite is true: Keno is in perfect working order and runs as smoothly as a Swiss timepiece, without ever having had any active instruction in timekeeping. He sees it as his task to show us very clearly on a daily basis how good he is at this. To the second. And this would awake great pride in his owner, you might think. But talking of awaking ...

At 6.45am on the dot, there is the first movement from my dog's basket; at 6.50am I have a sloppy wet dog's tongue in my face; at 6.55am, comes the first yowling "I-have-to-go-out-now-get-up" early morning call right next to my ear. The best thing about this is at 6.56am, I send Keno round to the other side of the bed, to do his special song for my husband, because since our son was born, I have been excused getting up to let the dog out in the morning. That's one of the benefits of motherhood.

However, Keno's internal clock keeps running accurately for the rest of the day, too. At 9.15am sharp he starts dancing around in front of the kitchen door because of his acute hunger pangs.

At 1.30pm he fixes his hypnotic stare on his mistress to try and detect the first signs of a walk in the offing. From 5.30pm he hangs around the front door expectantly, waiting for the return of his master. And finally at 8pm we are treated to Keno's determined attempts to be more interesting than anything that is on the TV. Very often the TV stays off and we cuddle up to his warm fur as a result of his efforts ... and very nice this is, too. As the clock strikes 9, however, our dog suddenly loses all enthusiasm for movement and stirs only to change position in his sleep. This regime doesn't vary even if we are away staying with other people. At midnight at the latest, Keno gets up and totters sleepily to stand in front of the bedroom door: "Come on you lot, time for bed." Ah well, who needs an alarm clock? The canine clock works perfectly.

To be honest, yesterday I would have been pleased if my watch had kept time as well as my dog, because instead of being exactly on time, as my watch told me I was, I was an entire big fat hour late for a meeting. Even Keno couldn't help with this one, as despite his great timekeeping skills, there is one aspect of time he has

never grasped: the way the clocks change in spring and autumn.

When the clocks change, Keno's internal clock is thrown into utter chaos for a couple of days. Basically, though, Keno would be the perfect, battery-free time check: "At the next bark, it will be 9.15am precisely and high time, therefore, that my bowl was filled." If it wasn't so completely out of fashion, he could have got a job as an announcer: "And now for our afternoon programme. We offer you an ambulatory demonstration of flora and fauna of field, forest and meadow, including two hours of fresh air and a free facial tanning session. Excellent entertainment!" No human could do it better!

Much as I am entertained, I do my best to ignore Keno's varied alarm clock-like requests. Every good book on dog training says "Do not allow your dog to dictate your daily routine." Exactly! Nevertheless, it is hard to deny my timelessly delightful dog his requests, because he is my very special programme highlight – 24 hours a day.

Leads off!

Skipping
Level of difficulty: ♡♡ to ♡♡♡
You will need: 1 lead about 3.5m long or 1 skipping rope, 1 person, 1 dog

How to do it
If you want to use your walks to improve your fitness in no time at all, whilst at the same time giving your dog a challenging new task, skipping is ideal. When I hit upon the idea, I tried it out immediately and found that I got very out of breath. When you have let your dog off the lead, cue him to sit behind you. Then take hold of the lead like a skipping rope in both hands, but stretch your left arm further out to the side to make space for your dog to jump with you. Initially, hold the lead low enough so that your dog – when you call him to you – first simply walks over it. After repeating this a few times, call your dog to you shortly before the rope swings up from the ground and you have to jump. Getting the timing just right requires a bit of practice, but when it works, it's really fun.

Variations on this theme
I'm not tremendously keen on playing too many games with the lead, and particularly not biting or tugging games. But I find it doubles really well as a skipping rope, simply because you always have it with you. You can stretch it out like a rope and get your dog to either jump over it or run underneath it. You could do this by clipping the karabiner to a fence or a thin branch, for example. This provides a bit of variety on a walk without having to carry anything extra.

Mountain climber
Level of difficulty: ♡♡ to ♡♡♡
You will need: 1 hill, 1 person, 1 dog, 1 toy

How to do it
Even in very flat areas, you can still find plenty of places that are ideal for this game; any slope will do. It's very easy to

make a hill running race out of this – up and down, up and down. Cue your dog to sit, run a little way up the hill/slope, then throw a ball or stick further up. Now release your dog to run after the toy and see who can reach it first! Turn around and play the game again going down the hill. An athletic way of getting off the beaten track and into the countryside.

Variations on this theme

You can also get your dog to follow a scent up and down the hill. Cue your dog into the 'down' position at the top of the slope, then take a zigzag course down the hill, leaving a few treats in prominent spots: this makes it easy for your dog if he is not used to scent-work. There are more scent-work ideas in the next chapter. We'll continue with the athletic theme here.

Hoopla
Level of difficulty: ♡♡ to ♡♡♡
You will need: Hula hoop, 1 person, 1 dog

How to do it
My mum still had my old red hula hoop from my childhood in her cellar (but for those of you whose mums have not kept your old toys, you can get these hoops very cheaply in virtually any toyshop!). I thought it might be useful for a game with Jaden and tried out all sorts of things. The first thing that came to mind was the classic jump through the hoop. First of all, familiarise your dog with the hoop – let him sniff it and give it a good look over. Then entice your dog through the hoop when it is standing upright on the ground (hold the hoop firmly with one hand). Hold a treat or a ball in your free hand and entice your dog through the hoop. After this, every time he goes through the hoop, hold it a little higher, until the necessary jump represents a reasonable challenge.

> *Hoopla*
>
> *1   First the classic jump through the hoop. Jaden is so keen that I could hold the hoop even higher.*
> *2   An alternative to the 'plain' hoop: I hang a cloth over the top edge of the hoop and get Jaden to jump through it.*

Variations on this theme
Try wrapping a variety of things around the hoop – a feather boa, cloths, the cardboard tubes from the insides of toilet paper rolls (cut them down one side and slide them onto the hoop) – or anything that you can find that will either flap or make a rustling sound. Long strips of crepe paper knotted onto the top of the

hoop look very effective – just like a trip to the circus!

Hula hoop
Level of difficulty: ♡♡ to ♡♡♡
You will need: 1 hula hoop, 1/2 people, 1 dog

How to do it
Yes, you read that right, we're still on hoops. For this game, it's really good if you can first teach your dog to circle you without the hoop; perhaps he has already learnt to do this at dog dancing or agility classes? Otherwise, you can quickly teach him to do a tight circle around one of your legs. Use treats to motivate him, and link the circling with a cue word such as 'round!' Then introduce the hoop, your hips and the athletic challenge to the

mix. 'Hula' the hoop around your hips whilst your dog circles your legs under the swinging hoop. This one will get you noticed!

Variations on this theme
With a helper, hold the hoop horizontally a little way off the ground. Ask your dog to step into the middle of the hoop. Increase the height of the hoop until your dog has to jump into the hoop. It's also fun to make the hoop roll until it falls flat on the ground and then give your dog the new cue for jumping into the hoop. If you have a water-loving dog, you can get him to jump from the bank or jetty through a hoop and into the water. An idea that is Jaden's own: he loves long-jumping over a horizontally-held hoop.

Hula hoop

1&2 Jaden sits behind me. When I call him, he walks through my legs whilst I hula the hoop around my hips.
3&4 Now I give him the cue for circling my legs. Phew! It's really not that easy to direct the dog and keep the hoop going.

Lead on!

Run with me
Level of difficulty: ♡ to ♡♡
You will need: 1 person, 1 dog on the lead, 1 toy

How to do it

Lead on, ready, let's go! Clip your dog's lead (it should be of 3.5m length) to his collar – or, preferably, his harness – and attach the other end to your belt or something similar. Joined like this you can run together – but if your four-legged friend is speedy, you can't let yourself be left behind. Cue your dog to sit, and then roll a ball a little way ahead of you – not too far, because you want to work on building up your fitness gradually. Step forward a couple of paces and cue your dog to run with you. Place your bets as to who gets to the ball first!

Variations on this theme

So what can you do when your dog has to be on a lead? Well, you can practice catching, for example. Begin with a very short distance between you and gradually increase this until you are right at the end of the (preferably extremely long) training

Run with me!

1   Golden Retriever, Nana, and her owner, Enno, are joined together by the lead and begin to run to the ball. Not a game for dogs that pull on the lead!
2&3 The very long lead enables them to play even with the lead on, and to play catch over increasing distances. You can see that Nana is athletic and wants to succeed. She manages to catch the ball first time. Good job!

lead. The smaller the item to catch, the more difficult the task of catching it. Worth a shot?

Stop and go
Level of difficulty: ♡♡ to ♡♡♡
You will need: 1 dog, 1 person, 1 lead

How to do it
Before you start running or walking with your dog at any pace, ensure that he will stop when you ask him to. When Jaden was on a long lead, I didn't want him constantly crossing the path in front of the children's pushchair, so used a very swift 'stop!' cue to deter him and get him to stand still. These days, I like to use the 'Stop and go' game when we are out for our Sunday morning jog (which I freely admit doesn't happen as often as it should!). Jaden is on a fairly long lead, and is either running abreast or a little way ahead of me. Suddenly, I say 'stop!' and then either 'sit!' or 'down!' and Jaden must stay in that position until I have gone ahead of him, when he is allowed to proceed – until the next 'stop!' The person has to keep moving for the duration of the game and the dog has to pay attention to see what is coming next. Not for couch potatoes!

Variations on this theme
You can also do this without a lead, but must be sure that your dog will do as you ask. Of course, you don't necessarily need the 'stop!' cue; you can go straight to 'down!' or not use any cue at all, but just keep changing the pace. Your dog has to pay attention and adapt his speed accordingly. This is quite difficult to start with, but becomes great fun for the two of you.

Get fitter!

1&2 The Beagles Anabel and Babette can be seen in alternate photos and also together. First, one has to balance along the angled board resting on a crate and then jump elegantly over the crate.

3 The two Beagles run through the chair corridors with ears flying.

4&5 The slalom: person and dog can go round the umbrellas together or the dog can be sent through by himself. Sabine and Babette demonstrate both. Impressive!

4

strenuous, no matter if you are on two wheels, two legs or four paws! And this is obviously something you can do with other dog lovers and their athletic furry friends – and maybe they will be able to contribute some interesting ideas for additions to this game. The core idea is that you construct an obstacle course and simply walk it with your dog. Then take your dog through/over the obstacles on the lead, whilst you cycle or run alongside him to keep up the pace.

Important! Before you take your dog through the entire course, familiarise him with each obstacle and practice it individually. Your dog also needs to be used to running on a lead alongside a bike or you before you start the course!

Obstacle course part 1
Lay a lead on the ground to indicate the start and finish line at the beginning of the course. After this, there is the first obstacle: the empty crate. Your dog must jump over this, whilst you run beside him. Of course, you can also send your dog ahead of you and then jump over the crate yourself. The level of difficulty can be increased by positioning two people next to the crate so that they can lift the crate off the ground; how high depends on the size and jumping ability of your dog. Straight after this, the dog (or dog and you, one after the other) must run through a corridor made of chairs or crates.

Obstacle course part 2
Next is the bench or the long wooden board, which your dog should quickly run across whilst you run alongside him on the ground. After this comes a slalom made of umbrellas (or poles) stuck into

5

the ground: these don't need to be lined up precisely – they can be positioned a little unevenly. (You need a lot of space between the poles to get a bike through!) After the last slalom post, turn around and race back to the finish line. Have a second run through the obstacle course, this time with dog and bike.

Variations on this theme
You can vary this game at any point just by adding new elements to the obstacle course. Give your imagination free rein and you will come up with any number of ideas. It adds an extra dimension to the course if you have to swop between walking, running and cycling when completing it. A challenge!

Running and cycling obstacle course
Level of difficulty: ♡♡♡♡
You will need: Dogs, people, a garden, empty country track or a field you can cycle on, 1 bike, 1 lead, 1 empty (bottle) crate and 2 to 4 chairs or more crates, 3 to 5 posts or umbrellas, 1 long board wide enough and strong enough for dogs to walk on, or a wooden bench, and a stopwatch for the very keen

How to do it
The extensive list above has already given the game away: this is going to be

Human obstacle course
Level of difficulty: ♡♡ to ♡♡♡
You will need: 1 dog, 3 people

How to do it

People today really put themselves out for their dogs! This game is ideal for nice warm days in the garden, the park, or on the beach. When it's really hot, always ensure you play in shady areas, and have plenty of water available for both people and animals.

Ask your dog to sit; he must wait until a human has positioned himself on all fours as a jump. If a higher jump is needed, hunch your back to make yourself higher. The second person also gets down on all fours but, in this instance, the dog has to run underneath. The third person accompanies the dog through the obstacle course to ensure that he does as he should. As soon as the dog has jumped over the first person and is running towards the second, the first person gets up and runs in front, positioning himself on all fours again, ready for the dog to jump over. This process can be repeated for as long as everyone's energy holds out!

Variations on this theme

The more people you have, the more things you can do. For example, you can have your dog run through your straddled legs, or jump over outstretched arms or legs. Perhaps you could also stand on your head and get your dog to jump through your legs. (If you manage to do the latter, please make sure you send me a photo; I'd really like to see that!) Whatever you organise, have fun and get the whole family involved.

Human obstacle course

1&2 An enterprising trio – mother, son and dog – who like trying out new things and demonstrating what they can do. When Katy gives the cue and the incentive, Buddy energetically jumps over Nick's back or runs under his stomach. Well done, guys!

The runway

1-3 The ball sits on the edge of the upturned crate. Jaden has to nudge it so that it starts moving and rolls down the run. Then Jaden is allowed to chase and catch the ball. A really self-rewarding game for your dog!

The runway

Level of difficulty: ♡♡♡ to ♡♡♡♡

You will need: 1 ball, a child's slide or a board balanced at an angle on a crate or similar, 1 dog, 1 person

How to do it

The challenge here is for the dog to get his ball to move by himself. Show your dog the ball and reward him when he touches it with his nose and moves it. Position the ball at the top of the board or the slide, but ensure that it won't move by itself. Encourage your dog to nudge the ball with his nose. The steepness of the slide will cause the ball to really gather speed so that your dog has to run after it to retrieve it.

Variations on this theme

You'll know you've really got this game cracked when your dog learns to replace the ball at the top of the slide after having retrieved it! A clicker would be beneficial for training such as this (see the section on clicker training in Chapter 7).

However, your dog may well be clever enough to work out for himself how to replace the ball. If that is the case, praise him, praise him, and then praise him some more!

very clever!

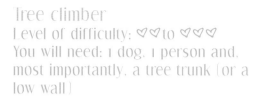

Tree climber

Level of difficulty: ♡♡ to ♡♡♡
You will need: 1 dog, 1 person and,
most importantly, a tree trunk (or a
low wall)

How to do it

Not earth-shattering news, I know, but it's
true: the woods really are a great place
to play. You can easily get off the beaten
track with your four-legged friend and

use any fallen tree to provide a challenge. But instead of jumping over the trunk in one bound, it's more stimulating for your dog if you can ask him to jump up on to the top and stay there. Whilst he's there, practice various cues such as 'sit' or 'shake,' or backwards walking. Get your dog to turn around on the narrow tree trunk, or throw him a ball to catch. This all constitutes good training for his sense of balance and physical confidence.

Variations on this theme
Keep your eyes open for opportunities and use whatever your immediate environment can offer. A tree stump can provide a small diversion, or you may come across something like a huge empty cable reel, onto which your dog can jump. It's also a joy to find hay bales in fields, or stacks of tyres ready for covering tarpaulins, which your dog can run over

or jump through. The point is that no two walks are ever the same.

Which one's the ball?
Level of difficulty: ♡♡♡♡
You will need: 1 person, 1 dog, several very different dog toys, a great deal of patience!

How to do it
This is quite a challenge for your dog. Begin with his favourite toy (maybe a ball?) Place this amongst two or three other toys, and ask your dog to 'fetch the ball!' If he finds the right thing, throw the ball for him. If he brings the wrong toy, don't comment, simply repeat the game. Once he's grasped this idea, select two or three very different toys. (For Jaden, I always take the ring, the ball and the Frisbee, or the rope.) Have your dog sit and wait whilst you place the three items some distance apart on the ground a few metres away from him. Then ask your dog to bring you a specific toy. As preparation for this game, get used to clearly mentioning each toy by name on a regular basis so that your dog can make the link between the toy and the word.

Variations on this theme
Simply lay out three or four toys and just ask your dog to bring you something, anything. Whatever he brings you, throw it for him or use it for a quick tugging game. After a while, hide this toy and ask for another, play with it, then hide it. Repeat until he has brought you all of the toys. By then, you will both have earned a break.

Something for the sports stars: check

√ Variety is the spice of life

√ Short, intensive bursts of exercise are preferable to daily long-distance endurance challenges

√ It's not about winning but about having fun. Be creative in building obstacle courses

√ Invite other people/dog teams to join in and have fun together

√ Include yourself in the game as much as possible - don't make your dog do things alone

√ You can have fun and keep up the pace even with your dog on a lead

Four paws & lots of brainpower: new thinking games for dogs

My dog's job ...
Glass painting
74

Free will instead
of duty-bound
80

Canine canniness
72

Try this!
76

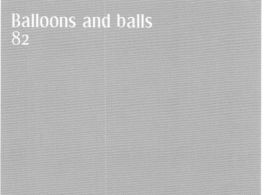

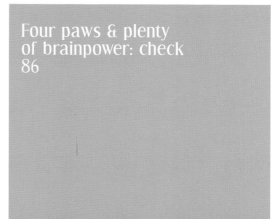

Canine canniness

"My dog understands me," say many keen dog owners. But does this mean that dogs understand things in the same way that we do? The wonderful author Jean Donaldson writes on this subject in what, for me, is her essential reference book – *The Culture Clash*: "When will we begin to see all the really fascinating things in dogs that make intelligence completely irrelevant? Dogs' ability to discriminate as displayed in classical conditioning; their scenting ability; their ability to cope in a complex social environment; their emotions and attachment to us – all of these are huge areas, about which much can be written. In comparison, only a very slim volume would be necessary to cover the extent to which intelligence plays a

Handy tip ♡

A suggestion!

When you are practicing little games and mental work with your dog, you don't always need to stick exactly to the rules as described in the book. Be open to suggestions from your dog. For example: maybe you want your dog to take socks out of a basket and bring them to you, but your dog drops the socks far away instead. Accept your dog's suggestion and practice 'sock dropping' instead. Often, you only notice just how many different ways an object can be used to have fun with when you have watched your dog in training. Let yourself be inspired by your dog.

Canine canniness

1   Clever or just cunning – how intelligent are dogs? Whichever is the case, they are undoubtedly consumate scent-workers.
2   When your dog has different ideas to you – about sitting still for the photographer, for example – accept it with good humour. Don't want to sit still, prefer to lie on your side? Renate laughs and gives a tummy rub!
3&4 Campino is only playing half-heartedly, so Tanja stops the game for a while; precisely the right thing to do!

Achieving fitness, little by little

Fitness is not only to do with muscles and stamina. Your dog should also build his fitness with exercises requiring mental exertion and concentration. In this respect, it pays to begin with lots of short practice sessions during the day, slowly and gradually increasing session length. And if find yourself asking: "It was going so well; why has my dog suddenly stopped focusing?" the answer is simply that he can't concentrate sufficiently any longer. He needs a break, so let him have one – right now!

Sheer brilliance ...

To teach our dog something, the method is very simple: ensure that the behaviour we want our dog to display has positive consequences for him. In other words, reward him – with attention, food, or a game. Clicker training does exactly this (see Chapter 7), and is incredibly helpful for successful, precise mental work with dogs – it's also lots of fun!

It really does pay dividends to discover exactly how dogs learn, even if you don't want to become an expert. As Jean Donaldson says: "Don't worry if it all seems much too complicated. In order to train dogs, you don't need to understand their learning behaviour and motivation perfectly. However, the more you do know, the easier training becomes." In some areas our dogs repeatedly surprise us with their very own special brand of creativity – which I write about in the following 'Interlude' – and which is mentioned in the Handy tip on the preceding page. Of course, this means that you and your four-legged friend are never going to run out of ideas!

part in all of this (and the same to cover human ability to sniff out bombs)." Yes, she means exactly what she writes, and all modern canine behaviour researchers and dog training experts agree with her.

Safe or dangerous?

A dog has no morals, no conscience; he doesn't make plans, nor seek revenge. He repeats successful behaviour and eventually drops behaviour that is ignored. He judges his environment solely according to whether it is safe or threatening. If what a dog does has

pleasant consequences, he will repeat it; if it has unpleasant consequences, he will avoid that behaviour in future. That's dog philosophy in a nutshell.

This does not mean that a dog is stupid, though, or is unable to learn: quite the reverse, in fact! You've probably known that for some time, but we dog owners have to remind ourselves that a dog functions in a completely different way to us, and therefore learns completely differently.

A dog will always be a dog, and never a human.

73

My dog's job ...

Glass painting

Splodges, petal-shaped, growing into fuzzy smears, all presented at knee-height: really modern painting doesn't involve colours, but turns everyday glass surfaces into a transcendent medium. Yep, you've read that right: my Keno is an artist, and in his professional creative efforts, my canine companion has developed his very own special brushstroke, executed by that ingenious tool nestling in the midst of his hairy beard; I mean, of course, his nose.

This extraordinary implement is kept constantly and perfectly damp by his pink tongue, which itself is dedicated to the execution of Keno's artistic performance. Empowered by these instruments, Keno gives himself artistic freedom to decorate the patio windows with new, grey smears at every opportunity – sometimes augmented by damp paw prints. His smudgy canine creations are displayed to best effect when the sun is low in the afternoon sky.

Which compels me – despite a humble admiration for my animal companion's genius, and even at the point, once, of going into labour – to grab a wet cloth and wipe away all traces of canine artwork. My suspicion was that not all of those who would later be coming to visit the baby would be appreciative of Keno's artistic efforts. I could just hear the disapproving voices of the new grandmothers: "Goodness, couldn't you have done something about your windows? Which mucky pup has been at work there?" So I regard my regular cleaning campaigns as animal protection, because nothing depresses or demoralises an artist more than unqualified denigration. Rejection cuts deep into the sensitive nature of the artist, particularly as Keno has long ago made a name for himself in this area. As far as I can tell from a human perspective, Keno is a real trendsetter in the world of dogs.

Yes, he certainly has a nose for new professional challenges. Whilst his fellow canines herd sheep, chase geese and accompany cattle across vast expanses of the American grasslands, he dedicates himself tirelessly to the search for employment with a starrier future ...

In order to make his canine friends aware of his artistic bent, Keno, cunning as ever, has designs on mobile advertising space: our car's rear windows. This marketing campaign, is, however, sabotaged by my husband, who now always prefaces any journey with the use of glass cleaner and cloth. He's more likely to drive off with no petrol in the tank than uncleaned windows.

In spite of this, word about this creative activity has spread so far around the canine community that I have now developed a special talent. With just one quick glance at the rear window, I can determine with 100 per cent certainty whether the car belongs to the owner of a dog nose painter. Maybe this unique talent will enable me to go on a game show, win lots of money, and then buy my insatiable artistic genius a huge stock of toys and treats, in the process also buying me a respite from window cleaning!

The truth is that Keno would be better off looking for a new job, though that – whatever it may be – will probably cause me grief, too. I really do think that as the canine big brother, he really ought to be more aware of his responsibility as role model to our young son, maybe choosing something more closely attuned to his natural tendencies of caretaker and minder. Chuck in a spot of wiping up here, a touch of tidying up there, and generally ensuring that a lot less hair is dropped, and you have the perfect job description! Which would also mean that the grandmothers wouldn't be able to complain about their granddog Keno, either.

Hmmm ...

Try this!

Bookmarking the paper
Level of difficulty: ♡♡
You will need: 1 dog, 1 person, a newspaper, various small dog toys, chewy strip

How to do it
Important note: printer's ink is poisonous to dogs, so ensure that yours does not chew the newspaper!

Now you need to hide something in the newspaper for your dog to find. Lay the open paper on the floor in front of your dog. Cue your dog to sit, and very obviously hide something underneath a sheet of newspaper. Give the cue for 'fetch' or 'seek.' Once he has understood the concept, hide small toys in several places throughout the paper. Your dog has to use his paws and nose to move the pages to find the toys and bring them to you. Whilst he is doing this, you have time to read the next game in this book. If you play this game with two dogs, you will notice that each has his own special 'technique.'

Variations on this theme
Lay narrow chewy strips in-between a few pages, with a small piece protruding out of the paper. Your dog has to pull out these bookmarks, one after the other.

Turn the page
Level of difficulty: ♡♡♡
You will need: 1/2 dogs, 1 person, an old newspaper or an old book, lots of thin cardboard strips, sticky tape

How to do it
Before picking up the newspaper or the old book, work with the cardboard strips initially. Hold out a cardboard strip to your dog. Encourage him to touch the end of the strip with his muzzle and to take it in his mouth and tug on it. The cue I use with Jaden is: 'try this!' which means that he should show me a variety of different things to do with an object. He gets a

Bookmark

1-4 As Jaden watches, I place a large toy between the pages of the newspaper; Jaden leafs through the pages to get it out.

Turn the page

1-3 I have stuck a narrow strip of cardboard into the TV guide. Prior to this, I let Jaden tug on a similar strip of cardboard. He does exactly the same now: he takes hold of the cardboard strip in his mouth, pulls, and turns the page!

treat for every 'suggestion' but a 'jackpot' of either an extra special tasty treat or a lot of treats when he comes up with the specific behaviour I am looking for. Using sticky tape, stick the cardboard strip onto a page of the newspaper, ensuring that the strip sticks out of the right-hand side of the page far enough for your dog to be able to grasp it. Encourage your dog again with your cue word or phrase. Keep a firm hold on the newspaper; if your dog is able to turn the page by pulling on the strip, give him lots of praise to let him know he's done exactly what you wanted him to.

Variations on this theme

Once your dog has understood that he is supposed to use the cardboard strip to turn the pages, make the challenge harder by laying down several newspapers with cardboard strips in them, or stick several cardboard strips into one newspaper. There's an excellent way for your dog to use this skill: if you stick the cardboard strips onto that day's page in the TV guide, your dog can open the magazine for you at the correct page! A trick that he will enjoy repeating every evening!

Cushion comfort
Level of difficulty: ♡♡♡ to ♡♡♡♡
You will need: 1 dog, 1 person, 1 low
stool, 1 cushion, lots of treats

How to do it

Show your dog the cushion and encourage him to do something with it: reward him if he picks the cushion up in his mouth and carries it. Next, place the cushion right beside the stool. Now, as soon as your dog has a corner of the cushion in his mouth, reward him every time the cushion touches the stool: the objective is to have your dog lay the cushion on the stool so that you can sit on it. Give a special 'jackpot' reward (see page 77) as soon as your dog places the cushion on top of the stool, irrespective of whether he does it by chance or on purpose. Decide on one or two cue words for this action; I use 'cushion' for fetching and carrying the cushion, and 'pad!' for putting the cushion on the stool.

Variations on this theme

Place the cushion on the floor and cue your dog into 'down' next to it. Then

reward him each time he places his head nearer the cushion. The aim is to have him lay his head right on the cushion.

Handy-work
Level of difficulty: ♡♡ to ♡♡♡
You will need: 1 dog, 1 pen, 1 person

How to do it
Concentrating on the details of the performance, even with simple games, increases the challenge for your dog, and, in this case, it's very precise handiwork.

Sit at your dining table, garden table or desk with a pen in front of you. Roll this pen slowly towards the edge of the table and off onto the ground. Now encourage your dog to pick up the pen in his mouth. Let your right arm hang loosely beside you and extend your right hand. Keep opening and closing your hand so that it attracts your dog's attention. Praise your dog when he approaches or touches your hand with the pen in his mouth. If he places the pen in your hand, he has earned himself a 'jackpot' (an especially large and tasty treat). Sometimes he has to place the pen in your right hand and sometimes in your left hand, regardless of the side on which you dropped the pen. As a desk worker, this is a game that comes to me particularly easily! Use a non-toxic child's felt tip pen for this game, not a pencil or crayon. Remember: the larger the pen, the easier the task.

Variations on this theme
When playing a game of ball, don't let your dog just put the ball down at your feet. Squat down as soon as he comes towards you with the ball in his mouth, and hold out both hands in front of you,

Cushion comfort

1-4 This looks really easy, but in fact took a lot of practice. Develop this game by training and practicing the individual steps: taking the cushion, bringing the cushion to the stool, placing the cushion on the stool, then sitting down, and giving your dog his reward.

Handy-work

1-3 Big dog/big pen. Renate has dropped the thick-barrelled pen on the ground. Babette picks it up. Renate holds out her hand and Babette places the pen in it. Perfect handiwork and perfect teamwork!

cupped like a bowl. Open and close your hands so that your dog gets the message that this is where he should deposit the ball. Only throw the ball again once it has been placed in your hands. Throwing the ball again acts as the reward in this case.

79

Freewill instead of duty-bound

Pacesetter
Level of difficulty: ♡♡ to ♡♡♡♡
You will need: 1 dog, 1 person, possibly
1 ball on a cord, lots and lots of treats

How to do it

These games involving legs start on quite
an easy level, but can be made as difficult
as you want (see *Variations on this
theme*).

For the first exercise, send your dog
through your legs. Stand in front of him
with your feet more than hip distance
apart. Hold the ball on a cord behind you
(so that the ball is visible through your
legs). Now encourage your dog to run
through your legs to get the ball. This is
the beginning of your 'pacesetter freestyle
set,' the exercises for which you and your
dog can run through one after the other,
keeping everything as fluid as possible.

Leg exercise 1

After the sprint through your legs, best
done with your back turned to your dog,
move on to the 'figure of eight.' So, your
dog has run through your legs from
behind and is standing in front of you.

Entice him to you and through and around
your straddled legs, so that he walks in a
figure of eight around them. Allocate a cue
word for this. I use 'eight,' and when Jaden
runs through my legs, the cue word I use
is 'bridge.'

Leg exercise 2

When he has completed the figure of
eight, cue your dog to sit on your left.
Bring your feet together whilst at the
same time conjuring some treats out of
your pocket. Then place your right leg in

Leg exercise 1

1-4 Sabine gets her Beagle to walk a figure of eight around her legs. She entices the dog around the 'course' with a treat in her hand. Once your dog has understood that he is supposed to walk around your legs and has linked this with a cue, you can stand upright and not reward until he has completed his figure of eight.

Leg exercise 2

1-3 Anabel crosses steps with Sabine by doing a walking slalom. Each time Sabine takes a step forward, Anabel walks under Sabine's leg. And as you can see from the way Anabel is looking up, Sabine is holding a treat ready as a reward.

front of you as if to step forward. With the treats in your right hand, entice your dog to cross in front of your left leg and behind your right leg. Whilst he does this, take another step so that he can do the same with the left leg. The cue word I use for

this is simply 'through.' After successfully completing a few leg slalom steps, stop and bring your feet together. To finish, your dog can now learn to walk around your legs when you are standing up straight with your feet together. You can generally quickly show the dog what you want him to do by getting him to follow your treat-filled hand around you. Link this with a cue such as 'round.'

Initially, practice each leg exercise by itself, independently to the other exercises. Then combine the four exercises. If you enjoy this, dog dancing offers plenty of other moves which entail the dog concentrating completely on his interaction with you. And everything goes more smoothly when done to music!

Variations on this theme

You can, of course, try some real acrobatics. Lie on your back and do a shoulder stand (like in PE lessons at school). Then part your legs in a straddle. A second person should then encourage your dog to jump through your legs (but be careful of your face!).

Or assume a bridge or crab position so your dog can jump over you or run underneath. It's a good idea to do this after you have been exercising, as you will be nicely warmed up and the muscles will be looser.

Have fun!

Balloons and balls

the hula hoop. First of all, let the hoop rest upright on the ground, and then try it with the hoop held off the ground a little way; this is really difficult. In fact, Jaden hasn't managed to do this yet, but really enjoys practicing!

Variations on this theme

Attach a cord to the balloon. Reward your dog for taking the cord in his mouth and causing the balloon to move. Now encourage him to jump through the hoop with the cord in his mouth. Then tie two or three balloons onto the single cord and get your dog to jump through the hoop again. And if you manage this, please take a photo of it and send it to me! My email address is inside the front cover of the book.

> *Airy-fairy*
>
> *1&2 It's no good trying to play with floating balloons outdoors, as we found out during this photo shoot. However, the Rhodesian Ridgeback, Snickers, demonstrates a way you can play with balloons in the garden. Simply tie a cord to the balloons and encourage your dog to run after and take hold of the end of the cord as the balloons float along.*

Airy-fairy
Level of difficulty: ♡ ♡ ♡
You will need: 1 balloon, hula hoop, 1 dog, 1 person

How to do it
Your dog will already be familiar with the hula hoop from the 'Off the lead' section: now you can help him really aim high! In order to do this, you will use a balloon, which your dog has to push with his nose, but please intervene at once should your dog start to use his mouth and teeth when playing with a balloon. You must only reward him when he uses his nose on the balloon. And now, here's the challenge: your dog has to push the balloon through

Halfway house
Level of difficulty: ♡ ♡
You will need: 1 ball (or other toy for retrieving), 1 dog, 1 person

How to do it
The idea behind this game sounds completely simple, but my dog finds it very difficult, no matter how often we play it. The game consists of you throwing the ball (or some other toy that your dog likes to retrieve), and getting your dog

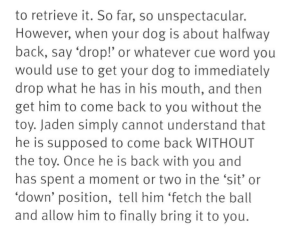

to retrieve it. So far, so unspectacular. However, when your dog is about halfway back, say 'drop!' or whatever cue word you would use to get your dog to immediately drop what he has in his mouth, and then get him to come back to you without the toy. Jaden simply cannot understand that he is supposed to come back WITHOUT the toy. Once he is back with you and has spent a moment or two in the 'sit' or 'down' position, tell him 'fetch the ball and allow him to finally bring it to you.

Variations on this theme
I can think of two other ways to play this

game. Your dog has to wait in the 'sit' or 'down' position until the ball has come to rest after you have thrown it. Then you send him to fetch it. Or, when your dog reaches the ball and picks it up, he has to wait in a 'down' position with the ball in his mouth until you call him to come to you. Keep switching between the different retrieving variations as this ensures that your dog is always attentive and keeps concentrating. It is a completely different challenge to the eternal cycle of throw-retrieve-throw-retrieve, as the dog has to use his brain – and listen very carefully to the cues.

crate crazy!

Don't lose your bottle!
Level of difficulty: ♡♡♡♡
You will need: 1 bottle crate with some
empty plastic (NOT glass!) bottles,
1 dog, 1 person, lots of treats

How to do it
Take all of the bottles out of the crate, bar
one. Now call your dog and cue him to 'try
something!' The objective is for your dog
to take the empty bottle out of the crate
and then put it back again, but at this
stage just let him do what he wants with
it. By lifting the bottle a little yourself, and
touching it to your dog's muzzle, gradually

Don't lose your bottle!

*1-4 Jaden demonstrates how to put the
bottle I have given him in the crate. He
finds it significantly easier to fetch a bottle
from an otherwise empty crate and bring it
to me.*

*In both cases you will require a great
deal of patience and your dog will need to
really use his brain.*

King of the box

*1&2 Buddy shows how bright he is. He's
out on a walk and has come across his toy
box; he immediately looks for his ball in
there – what a little champion!*

introduce the idea of his taking the bottle in his mouth and lifting it from the crate to bring to you. Make sure you reward every effort he makes towards the objective, and use an appropriate cue word (such as 'lift') every time he does so that he associates the word with the action (and the reward!). You will notice that you need an enormous amount of treats for this game – particularly when getting your dog to return the bottle to the crate – because it is really difficult. But wouldn't it be good if your dog could stash your empty plastic bottles for you?!

Variations on this theme

Fill an empty plastic bottle (the inside of which is completely dry) with small, round treats and leave the top off. (Use a bottle made of really strong plastic.) Show your dog how treats fall out of the bottle and then give it to him: does he get the treats out? This is a really good activity for when your dog is alone at home.

King of the box
Level of difficulty: ♡♡ to ♡♡♡
You will need: 1 cardboard box, 1 dog, 1 or 2 people, 1 favourite dog toy

How to do it
First an old game – and then a new one.

In a cardboard box hide something of your dog's and have him find it and take it out, or you could teach him to jump into the box and lie or sit in it. This is a quick and easy game to have fun with whenever an online shopping delivery means the arrival of a large cardboard box. However, you can put a new spin on playing with

cardboard boxes if you bring yourself into the game. So, YOU hide in a large cardboard box and have your dog look for you (obviously he has to wait in another room whilst you are hiding). Or hide your dog's favourite toy in the cardboard box. With the box in the same location, tell him to 'find your toy' a few times.

Then do a test to determine whether your dog has understood that his toy is in the box. Take the box into a different room, and tell him again to find his toy: does he go straight to the box? If so, your dog has made the connection that the toy and the box belong together and will be enjoying a sense of achievement.

Variation on this theme
Give your dog an old towel (or a rolled-up pair of socks). If he takes the item to the

box, reward him with treats. The aim is for your dog to put two or three items – which you have previously strewn around the room – into the box. If your dog does all this and more, then I take my hat off to the king of the box!

Four paws and plenty of brainpower: check

√ Dogs really are multi-talented!

√ Dogs learn by their successes - praise, games and treats all represent success to a dog

√ Allow your dog to try as much as possible for himself

√ Give clicker training a go! It's great fun and accelerates learning in all mental games

√ The best motivators are a favourite toy and favourite treats

√ Brainwork is the hardest type of work for you both, so don't forget to take regular breaks!

The little ones can join in, too; have fun, Kids!

Yes, kids can join in!
90

Rainy days
92

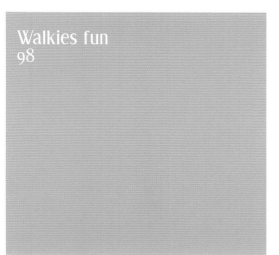

Walkies fun
98

Children's birthday party
101

The little ones can join in:
check
106

Yes, kids can join in!

1-3 The young Rhodesian Ridgeback Snickers lives in a large family with three lively children. He certainly benefits from this, as he is definitely never bored. And the children benefit, too, because when they play together, dog and child become a team, and the dog is a playmate and not a toy.

Hey, kids; what's going on here? Running around the garden, playing in the house, or discovering nature on daily dog walks is not for couch potatoes (see Handy tip). There's a good reason why the subject of games for dogs and children has a chapter all to itself, and it's because I keep getting new ideas for it. My offspring are still young and, right from the start, I wanted children AND a dog, as this is my idea of a 'dream team' which guarantees fun and happiness for the whole family.

A child-friendly dog is a safe dog!

If a dog is to play with a child it's obviously important that he is safe to do so and easy to manage. As you will notice with almost all types of game, a well-trained dog is the basic prerequisite for having fun together.

Handy tip ♡

Team-mates!

Dogs are not toys, but they do make great playmates for children. If you notice that children are trying to treat your dog as though he is a toy, choose a game in which the children and the dog have to work together to achieve something. Start with simple retrieving: for children who don't have much contact with animals, it's a really magical feeling when the dog brings them something. Or when they stand with their legs apart and the dog runs through them. Or when they jump over a tree trunk together. Then this four-legged creature becomes their partner – and perhaps their friend.

At the same time, in my experience, right from the start you also have to explain clearly to the little ones what they can and cannot do with the dog. Children quickly work out that their parents tell the dog what to do and what not to do. They find this fascinating and enjoy testing out this power that humans have over animals, but I do not allow the children to be in charge of the dog.

A dog should sit if asked to by the children, but I do not allow any situations to develop where my youngsters might have total responsibility for managing Jaden, which means that I always supervise play sessions. Of course, this situation changes as children get to school age, but a child should never have sole responsibility for any animal. If a family acquires a dog, then the parents have primary responsibility for his care, and particularly for training. The children can help, and the older they are, the more they are able to.

Dogs can bite ...

A situation where a child is bitten by a dog

(and I'm not talking about cases where a particular type or breed of dog savages a child), could come about because children are often not given proper guidance about how to interact with dogs. This is why I make great efforts to give children a basic understanding of dogs – for example, I write a monthly article for the children's pages of my local newspaper. From the responses I get, it's clear to me

that children absorb all this information and then have real moments of insight when they next meet a dog. An example of this is the wagging tail. The general concensus is that, if a dog is wagging his tail, he's happy and pleased to see you, but we should also be aware that a slowly wagging motion, with the tail held very erect, is a clear message to "Stay away from me!" Misunderstandings are simply inevitable if both parents and children believe that a wagging tail always equals a friendly dog. If, in this situation, the dog then growls or snaps, both children and adults are bewildered. So, educate yourself and then tell your children – and their friends – what you know about dogs. Using play is an ideal way to do this, as every good, positive experience with a dog gives children a priceless insight to these wonderful, loyal creatures. Let your little children play with your dog – but safely!

Your dog can make you smarter!

These are not my words: I'm simply quoting from a press release. Robert Poresky, a psychology professor at Kansas State University, discovered that children who grow up with pets have a higher IQ. He said: "Children that do not have a pet in the home have an average IQ of 108. Those who have a pet have an average IQ of 115." And Professor Poresky also says: "If a child gets on with an animal, then he will generally also have no problems getting on with people." A survey carried out by Infratest Burke also shows that 61.2 per cent of the people surveyed are certain that children who live with animals are happier. I am certainly happy to be a member of this particular majority group!

Rainy days

Treat detectives
Level of difficulty: ♡♡
You will need: a dark room, a torch (or maybe two), treats, 1 child (or more), and 1 dog, a simple puzzle

How to do it
The dark is good for hiding in, or scaring people, or enjoying a really fun game involving the sense of smell, and the most important item of equipment that a detective can have: a torch. Play this very special indoor game on a dark, rainy day. It's very simple, but I bet it's also completely different from anything else you may have played with your dog and your child!

With the light on, strew some treats around a room. Then turn the light out and invite the children and dog into the room to search for the treats. The aim is for the children to use the torch to find the treats before the dog sniffs them out. Whoever finds the most treats before the dog has eaten them can hide the treats for the next game. Be careful that your dog doesn't get too good at this or he will start to put on weight!

Variations on this theme
You can hide treats for the dog and pieces of a puzzle for the children. The children have to use the torch to find the pieces of the puzzle and put it together whilst the dog searches for his treats, just using his nose. Once the puzzle is completed, the dog has to stop searching; who will finish first?!

Sock it to me!
Level of difficulty: ♡♡
You will need: old socks, lots of children's feet, rewards for your dog

How to do it
Have the children sit in different corners of a room and wiggle their feet, on which they are wearing short socks, pulled just

a little way over their toes (the better your dog becomes at this game, the further up you can pull them). One by one, the children call the dog to them and let him pull off their socks (you will need to give a cue, such as 'pull,' and perhaps touch a sock to your dog's mouth initially so that he gets the idea). The kids really enjoy this, particularly when the dog has to pull really hard and it tickles their feet. For each pair of socks the dog manages to remove, he gets a treat from the child, and then the next child calls him over, and so on. So that no one becomes bored whilst they are waiting their turn, you could sing a song. And what should you sing? Well, that's obvious: "You put your right leg in, your right leg out, in, out, in, out, shake it all about ..."

Variations on this theme

Staying with the footwear theme, instead of getting your dog to pull off socks, he can also (particularly if he is a small dog) learn to untie shoelaces. The thicker the shoelaces, the easier it is for the dog to grasp them, and he gets a reward for each lace that he unties. This game is also a great opportunity for your children to practice tying bows (something that is neglected these days when so many children's shoes fasten with Velcro).

off the child. If your dog manages this, it's grounds for celebration: from now on, your dog can get your children up every day!

Variations on this theme
Can your dog lie down on cue; perhaps even on his side as though sleeping? Have your dog in the 'down' position and use the cue 'sleep' whilst covering him with a small, lightweight blanket (one of his own, if possible). If he stays lying quietly with the blanket on him, reward him. Then encourage him to 'pull' on the blanket; leave it up to him how he does this. Reward every attempt to do something with the blanket. Eventually, he will pull it off, at which point, produce a 'jackpot' reward and congratulate your clever dog.

Time to wake up, children!

1&2 First of all, I 'explained' the basic principle of the game to Jaden by pulling gently on a corner of the blanket. Then I placed the blanket over the children's legs. When Jaden tries to pull away blanket, the children hold the blanket for a short time to make it a little more difficult for Jaden, after which he manages to pull it completely off their legs, much to their delight.

Ball track bigwig

1&2 A game which demands a high level of concentration from the dog, and very exact timing of praise. Jaden demonstrates taking the wooden ball from my hands and placing it at the top of the track.
3&4 The ball has arrived at the bottom and Jaden collects it carefully and places it back in my hand. I am delighted that it worked!

Time to wake up, children!
Level of difficulty: ♡♡♡
You will need: 1 small blanket, 1 dog, at least 1 child

How to do it
Show your dog a small blanket and temptingly wave a corner of it under his nose, as if inviting him to a tugging game. If he takes hold of and pulls on a corner of the blanket, reward him. Once he has repeated this a couple of time, move to step 2. For this, the child sits or lays on the ground and covers himself with the little blanket. Now encourage your dog to 'try something' with the blanket. If he takes a corner in his mouth and pulls again, reward him, at the same time, giving the 'pull' cue. The aim is for the dog to pull hard and long enough on the blanket (and step backwards or sideways a few paces) for it to come right

Ball track bigwig

Level of difficulty: ♡♡♡♡
You will need: an old wooden ball
track, 1 child, 1 dog

How to do it

Have you an old ball track lying neglected
in a corner somewhere? Well, put it to
good use and let your dog play with it!
The ball tracks for very small children are
ideal, as the wooden balls and other items
for rolling down the track are nice and big.

Position a ball right next to the track,
and reward your dog if he picks it up in his
mouth. With your dog standing in the right
place, ready to let go of the ball, you and
the children must watch very attentively,
and say 'drop!' at the very moment he
drops the ball (which, hopefully, will fall
onto the track and roll down it). Even if
this doesn't happen first time, reward your
dog for approaching the ball track, and
particularly for touching the upper part
of the track with the ball in his mouth.
As soon as your dog drops the ball in the
right place, give him a big reward.

Variations on this theme

You can simplify the game by putting the
balls in a corner of the room, and ask your
dog to fetch the balls and bring them to
the child to use on the ball track. Or ask
him to collect the balls from the bottom of
the track and return them to the child.
Just experiment!

95

Hide and squeak

Level of difficulty: ♡♡
You will need: 1 dog and 1 squeaky dog toy per child

How to do it

Here's a little hide and seek game for dogs and children. The children should hide somewhere in the garden or house. Then send your dog to look for the children. In order to encourage the dog to seek, the children should squeak the dog toy from time to time, which will motivate your dog to look absolutely everywhere.

Variations on this theme

To make it harder for your dog, have your children hide without a squeaky toy. Or, hide your dog, rather than the children, with either a new or favourite squeaky toy. The children then have to close their eyes, listen and guess which room or part of the garden the dog (who should be investigating his squeaky toy!) is in. The children have to first say where they think the dog and his squeaky toy is hiding, and are then allowed to go and search the room or area they have named. If the dog is not there, they have to close their eyes again and listen carefully to determine exactly where the dog is hiding.

Hide and squeak

1-3 "Where are you?" When a dog is searching, he is using his sense of sight, but reacts much more strongly to scents and sounds. So the hider uses the ball's squeak to give the dog a clue and Snickers soon finds his young friend. The reward that he really enjoys is when the ball is thrown or kicked really far for him to chase after.

1

2

3

Message in a bottle
Level of difficulty: ♡ ♡ ♡
You will need: 1 hard plastic bottle, children or child and parents, 1 dog, pens and paper

How to do it
One child draws a picture or writes a short message for the other child or for his parents. The sheet of paper is then rolled up and the picture or the message is hidden in the empty plastic bottle (the smaller the dog, the smaller the bottle!). Then it's time for the dog to do his bit. The child calls the dog and tells him to carry the bottle. Then he is either sent to the other person, or the other person calls the dog. The dog must give the bottle to the person who has called him, and receives a reward for being the postie.

Before you start playing this game, practice getting your dog to carry a plastic bottle. Also practice getting him to run to the person whose name he hears.

Variations on this theme
If your dog is too small to carry a bottle, or doesn't want to carry something like this in his mouth, wrap a thick piece of cord or string around the neck of the bottle and tie it securely. He can then pull the bottle along by the cord. On hot summer days, you can also throw a tightly closed bottle into water for your dog to retrieve by taking hold of the cord.

walkies fun

Ring-a-ling
Level of difficulty: ♡♡
You will need: 3 or more rings, 10 to 20cm in diameter), children, 1 dog, lots of treat

How to do it
This requires a little scent-work from your dog, though it's really mainly about making the daily dog walk more fun for the children. Take a few small flat rings

with you (the children can make these themselves out of paper or cardboard, cutting them out and colouring them in). On the walk, as soon as you reach a quiet field or woodland track, send the children ahead with the rings and treats. Their job is to place the rings along – or slightly off – the path with the treats in the middle. The dog must then put his nose to work, sniffing out the tasty treats; the rings will help him to visually find the treat stops.

Variations on this theme
Your dog must sit and stay whilst you draw a line on the path. Place the rings on the ground a little way ahead of the line. From behind the line, the children have to throw the treats so that they land inside the rings. When all of the rings each contain a treat, your patient dog can run and get his ringed quarry.

Own goal
Level of difficulty: ♡♡
You will need: at least 1 child and 1 dog

How to do it

The love of animals unites people, don't you think? This premise forms the basis for this new game, because you and your child have to hold onto each other in order for your dog to try out something new.

Create the 'own goal' by simply holding hands to form a large vertical circle. Whilst you get into position, ask your dog to 'sit' until you give him the cue to jump. Start off by keeping the circle that you make with your arms very close to the ground, and gradually increase the height of the jump, depending on your dog's size and skill. If you have more people, they can also make circles with their arms, and your dog can do several jumps, one after the other.

Variations on this theme

It's possible to build a human obstacle course with children, and get your dog to jump through arms, over legs, run through legs, or jump over several children lying on the ground (obviously tailor this to how well the dog can jump – and get the children to lie face down!). Or one child can run the dog around a slalom course where other children are the slalom poles. This is a great way of reducing a fear of dogs in a child without him or her having to stroke or directly touch the dog.

an especially tasty treat deep into the boot toe; your dog will be so engrossed sticking his nose into the boot in an effort to get at the treat that he will barely notice the cleaning and grooming going on.

Christmas stocking
Level of difficulty: ♡♡
You will need: 1 small child's Wellington boot, treats and children

How to do it
Take a child's worn-out Wellington boot and fill it with treats (if your dog has a short muzzle, stuff the boot with some newspaper first. Show the boot to your dog and let him sniff it so that he knows the treats are inside.

Then give the boot to your children and begin the walk. At some point along the way, the children should run ahead and hide the boot, telling the dog "find the boot!" A Wellington boot works particularly well because it can be used in all weathers, can be wedged between branches and in bushes, and is large enough so as to be easily found.

Variations on this theme
This can also be a useful tool for keeping your dog in one place; whilst you are brushing or drying him, for example. Push

children's birthday party

Give and go
Level of difficulty: ♡♡ to ♡♡♡♡
You will need: children, 1 dog and 1 ball/toy

How to do it
A dog who is very used to and safe with children is ideal for this game in which kids are going to be moving around. You will need one dog toy that the children will find easy to throw and the dog likes retrieving.

To prepare for this game, practice the 'give!' cue with your dog, so that he will place the toy directly in your hands. Squat down and cup your hands together for this. Important note: only throw the toy again once the dog has really properly placed it in your hands.

Then it gets more difficult: the children stand spread out in the garden. One of the kids throws the toy, which the dog retrieves. The child squats down, calls the dog to him, cups his hands and lets the

dog place the toy there. Then he throws the toy to another child, who throws it for the dog, and receives it back in the same way. The dog must always take the toy to a different person each time. Will he manage it? Try it and see!

Variations on this theme
You can make this more difficult by changing the person to whom the toy is taken, ie the dog has to take it to a child other than the one who threw it. Call out a child's name after the toy is thrown, who should then squat down to accept the toy. And the children don't stay standing still, as, whilst your dog is running after the ball, they can run around too. Great fun!

Give and go

1   I cup my hands together. Bastian does the same with his and puts them above mine. (I previously practiced the 'give!' cue with Jaden so that he understands this as the signal to put the toy straight into my cupped hands.) Jaden puts the toy into our hands. The next time, Bastian manages it by himself and we can begin playing the game!

in 'Give and go,' for example. The children stand in two rows, facing each other. This creates a passageway between them for the dog, who waits at the beginning of the archway. The birthday boy or girl stands at the other end of the archway and uses the cue 'come!' or 'here!' to get the dog to run through the archway to him. Once the dog has done that, the first caller takes the place of the first child in the arch and the last child then has a turn at calling the dog to come back through the archway. Every couple of times this happens, reward your dog in some way, otherwise he is not getting anything for his efforts! This game is easy for your dog, but may prove a test of courage for some of the young guests.

Variations on this theme

The game begins as detailed above, but with one difference: the birthday boy calls the dog, but stands behind one of the sides of the archway and taps one child on the shoulder. This child has to quickly place their feet far apart, whilst the birthday boy or girl entices the dog through the other child's legs and out of the archway. Don't have the children stand in a circle around the dog, though, as he may find this intimidating.

Archway
Level of difficulty: ♡♡
You will need: children, 1 dog.

How to do it
Children's birthday parties can sometimes feel very long, and there are some children who are anxious about dogs because they aren't used to them. In this game, you help the children make an archway for the dog. Children who are frightened of dogs can usually also participate, as they don't have to actually touch the dog as they do with taking the ball from the dog

Dog and pot

Level of difficulty: ♡♡ to ♡♡♡
You will need: 1 plastic pot, maybe a sieve, 1 wooden spoon, 1 child, treats

How to do it

There are three versions of this game for dogs: novice, expert and professional.

Novice: The dog sits and watches whilst the child hides a piece of sausage under a sieve. The dog is then told 'find it!' and has to sniff out the treat under the sieve, either pushing away or turning over the sieve to get at the piece of sausage. (The sieve makes the game easier as the dog can sniff the treat through the holes.)

Once the dog has understood how the game works, you can try hiding the treat under a plastic pot.

Expert: The dog waits in the house, or in the next room whilst the child or children put out several plastic pots upside-down on the lawn or on the floor. Hide a treat under one pot only. Will your dog's nose be keen enough for him to find the right pot straightaway?

Professional: If you have a dog who really likes a challenging game, give him a wooden spoon to hold in his mouth which he must use to tap the pot before he can turn over the pot and eat the treat.

Dog and pot for novices

1&2 Jaden waits and watches whilst I place the sausage under the sieve – then he can get it!

Dog and pot professionals

3&4 The dog takes a wooden spoon in his mouth, which he must use to touch the pot before he can get to the treats.

103

This version requires a lot of practice and you need to break it down into sections: holding the spoon in your dog's mouth, touching something with the spoon, then turning over the pot.

Variations on this theme

The children place treats in plastic cups and float them in the water. Your dog has to carefully lift out each cup and tip the treats out onto the ground.

Ship snacks

Level of difficulty: ♡♡♡

You will need: 1 plastic boat that floats well, a small bowl of water, large and small treats (eg chewy strips and dog biscuits)

How to do it

No children's party in the summer should be without a paddling pool. And our four-legged friends can have some fun in there too, with 'ship snacks,' for example.

Fill a small tub or a large bowl three-quarters full with water. The edge of the bowl should be low enough for your dog to reach everywhere within the bowl. As a practice, first throw a few treats into the bowl for your dog; small pieces of chewy strip float really well. The dog then has to fish them out.

This is a refreshing little exercise, but be warned: if your dog gets his ears wet, he will undoubtedly shake himself straight after finishing this game.

Float a few boats in the dog play pool, and have the children place a large treat such as a dog biscuit or a piece of sausage on to each boat. After this, the dog is allowed back to the pool again. Will he sink the boats while getting the snacks?

Variations on this theme:
The children place treats in plastic cups and float them on the water. The dog lifts each cup out of the water and tips them over to get at the treats.

Ship snacks

1   Two boats are each laden with a big treat. Jaden carefully unloads the food.
2   There are now paper cups bobbing in the water. Jaden gets hold of the edge of the cup with his teeth in order to 'land' it and tip out the tasty contents.

Visit Hubble and Hattie on the web: www.hubbleandhattie.com and www.hubbleandhattieblogspot.com
Details of all books • New book news • Special offers • Gift vouchers

105

The little ones can join in, too: Check

√ Be sensitive in dealing with a child's fear of dogs

√ Keep unsettled children and unsettled dogs apart

√ Explain to children how dogs behave

√ Establish rules about how the dog should be treated

√ Whenever a child is playing with a dog, he or she should always be supervised by an adult

√ Children enjoy going on walks which incorporate games

√ Your dog is part of the family, so do as much as you can together

A break in play: thinking about dog training

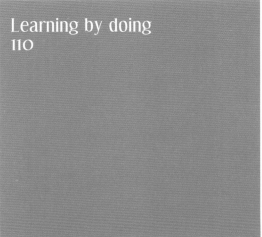

Click, click, hooray!
116

Time to rest, finally
118

A break in play: check
120

Learning by doing

Yes, my motto for life with dogs is "learning by doing." For me, this means you learn with and from your dog. I read many, many dog books before Jaden came to live with us as a puppy. I knew everything there was to know about the theory – about socialization, training and how to live with a dog. And then Jaden came along. Much of the theory was put into practice, and some things that I had not read anywhere were put into practice, too. I discovered that every dog owner has to consider what advice and information about dogs is available, and choose the bits that work for him or her in everyday life. I tried out a lot of stuff and discarded some of it. I wrote about what worked for me in my introductory book on dog training: *Train your dog – the relaxed way*: here's a short summary of the fundamental ideas.

Being a dog lover means doing some mental work!

I am completely convinced that humans (including children and neighbours!) and dogs can really only live together successfully when the human has a sound knowledge of dog behaviour and how dogs learn. As we are in control of the lead, we determine whether or not the human-dog team works, because dogs are happy to follow our lead, except when they feel that we are uncertain or unreliable. Dogs need clear guidelines,

clear communication, and unambiguous (body) language, because a dog is a dog and not a human. So we must tell him clearly and simply what we want from him.

Off to school?

Perhaps you won't manage to get everything in this book to work, but your dog is worth you making every effort to understand him, get on with him and commit to his welfare and well-being. Of course, sometimes there are situations where no book can provide the answers. In this case, investigate dog training schools and clubs for dog owners; there are bound to be some good ones somewhere in your locality where you will find trained experts who will help you get the most from life with your dog.

Keep communicating!

Living and being with your dog is always about co-operation, and similar to a dialogue. Use your knowledge about how your dog learns, what motivates him, the timing of praise and, in particular, your knowledge of his (body) language. Then you can enter into a real dialogue with your dog and he will understand you – even without words. Here, I can quote from my own text: "Of course, you can't really converse with your dog. If, however, you understand how a dog processes new information, and how to establish a particular behavioural reaction, then you have achieved the same amount as a teacher would have in an intensive lesson in school."

1-5 *Playing together, working together, belonging together. With her Giant Schnauzer, Macho, Gaby demonstrates all the good sides of living with dogs. She and Macho have regular intensive training sessions; they are an enthusiastic and successful retrieval team, and are equally good at relaxing and having a cuddle. Ultimately, you and your dog should be a good fit!*

Handy tip ♡

Play and stop!

Many dog owners refuse to use what they see as 'treat bribery;' is this a view that you share? If so, practise using a 'reward game' with your dog. This entails briefly producing a special toy that your dog especially likes to play with, playing for a few minutes then ending the game and carrying on with the exercise. My dog is a treat dog. After a quick play with a ball or a Kong™, his concentration is lost, so you probably need to introduce a reward game at a very early stage. Another tip about using treats as rewards: over time, reduce the amount of treats you give so that eventually they only appear sporadically.

what is going on inside your dog's head?

A dog's most important attribute is that he is a pack animal; a 'four-legged family man,' if you will. That doesn't mean, however, that you should spend as much time as possible with your dog, but you can safely assume that a dog is looking to interact with his social partner. And as any exchange (we would say 'talking') amongst dogs takes place almost exclusively via body language, a dog is a very astute observer; of people, specifically.

He analyses and interprets all of our movements as well as our voice, always based on the question: is this situation safe or unsafe for me, and does this behaviour mean that there will pleasant or unpleasant consequences for me?

Hey, I get you!
So, knowing that our dog is observing us, we need to use cues that are completely unambiguous for him. As dogs don't deal in words, it will help him if you use your body when communicating: for example, instead of just saying 'sit!' use a visual cue also, such as a raised index finger; instead of just calling 'come!' use a beckoning

gesture at the same time. This makes it much easier for your dog to immediately understand what you want him to do and dispenses with any ambiguity.

Dog meets dog
From now on, as an incentive to reassess your behaviour towards your dog and to begin the dialogue with your four-legged companion on a new basis, pay close attention to every off-lead meeting between canines. Don't make the mistake

Dog meets dog

1&2 When two dogs meet, you can see very clearly how they 'talk' to each other using their body language. Watch their tails, ears, and the position of their heads. Both dogs are addressing each other in a polite, friendly and obviously peaceful manner. You can see this from the way they are lowering their heads and making themselves smaller. The photos also show that the dog which is sitting down has the upper hand in the situation as the other dog is approaching him. He also ends the encounter by leaving, which translates as "Nice meeting you – bye!"

of thinking that the signals which pass between them begin when they are sniffing each other, or playing; if you look more closely you will see that the signs begin when the dogs are still many metres away from each other. They watch one another; wait; sniff at the edge of the path; lie down; turn away, turn around to the other dog. These rituals have an important meaning: dogs can determine a great deal from some distance away, because they look very closely at how the other dog is behaving. Is he lowering his head in a friendly manner, or is he holding up his tail aggressively? Does he appear calm and at ease, or is his body language ambiguous or immature?

We can learn a lot about how to deal with our dog from observing these

greeting signals, or calming signals, as they are known. For example, it's impolite to approach the other party head-on, so if you call your dog to you and he approaches you from the side, then you know that he's being polite and friendly. From observing what dogs do when they meet each other, we also learn that you shouldn't look animals you don't know in the eye, or bend over them, or touch them from above. A better way to do it would be to squat down beside a strange dog, with your face slightly averted, to say a friendly "Hello!"

Whatever we two-legged creatures are trying to teach our dogs, it always means the same thing to the dog: he has to learn something. Luckily, dogs really love to learn; of course, some breeds are keener in this respect than others, but generally, dogs are straightforward and really pleased when we are happy because something has worked. So, just how does a dog learn?

I will endeavour to cover the essential key elements here, but please feel free to take this opportunity to read as many books as you can on this subject. I am always reaching down dog books from my bookshelf and leafing through them; even when I am very familiar with them, dipping into them again often brings new insights. And for this reason I am always inclined to listen to experts when they are saying something about my dear friend, the dog.

The benefit: success!

Dogs want one thing: their behaviour

to result in success, and something pleasant to happen after. If they get the best possible outcome, they will repeat the behaviour in the hope that the same will happen again! In order to achieve a positive result, dogs are very creative

and will try a wide range of different behaviour: this is known as trial and error learning, and learning through success.

When you are playing with or training your dog, you can make excellent use of this basic principle. Because we know pretty much exactly what a dog regards as success – attention, food, or when he gets to walk further on the lead or go where he wants to go – we can ensure that these things happen as a result of the dog's behaviour. For example, if your dog walks nicely on the lead, you praise him, and maybe give him a treat. The dog observes: "if I walk next to the human like this, things that I like happen." He will then very probably repeat the behaviour. If he immediately experiences success again, he will incorporate walking next to his human as part of his standard behaviour. And you can achieve this simply through being consistent and having a good understanding of dogs!

Learning, not unlearning!

If you don't praise a desirable behaviour for a long time, you may end up unintentionally erasing it, because if a behaviour is not rewarded, the dog will unlearn a particular game or exercise, so remember to sporadically praise your dog for all the things at which he is very good. Attentive readers will have already worked out my favourite saying: always notice when your dog does something right!

Click, click, hooray!

action and the immediate reaction and consequence, and actually does this in an instant. For example, your dog sits down and you give him a treat immediately; he associates his action with the pleasant consequence. If you also use the cue 'sit!' he links that to the event also and learns: "If I sit down when I hear 'sit!' I get something nice. It's worthwhile, so I'll keep doing it!"

If we are slow with the praise and reward, and the dog has become distracted and even begun to lift his behind off the ground before the reward is given, then there is no association with the cue word, or we confuse him because

How do you teach a dolphin to jump through a hoop? Many years ago, Karen Pryor was wrestling with exactly this problem. She searched for a solution and came across the concept of 'operant conditioning,' a term devised by psychologist B F Skinner, which describes behaviour that has been reinforced by reward, or discouraged by punishment. In the case of the dolphin, before it could begin to learn a task, it had to recognise that every time a hooter was sounded, it was followed by a tasty fish. Clicker training for dogs, devised by Karen, is based on exactly the same principle. Her book *Don't Shoot the Dog!* is well worth reading. Check out the book for yourself; I guarantee you'll be surprised, impressed and enthused!

Click & reward - now!

Whether you watch "It's me or the dog," or go to a good dog training club, you will hear the same refrain from dog trainers – when it comes to operant conditioning, it all depends on timing. Why? Because it's to do with association. The dog learns by making a connection between his

Handy tip ♡

Treats come after!

Dog trainer and author Birgit Laser draws attention to a big advantage of clicker training: "Many of us are probably familiar with this scenario: your dog does everything you ask of him if you have a treat or a toy in your hand. But with clicker training, the dog learns that he has to do something before he even sees a treat." So the treats stay in your pocket until AFTER the click.

quickly than you can spell out the word: click and treat, click and treat, click and treat. It's important that the treats are very small and really need to be something that your dog can devour in one gulp.

A typical beginner's exercise in using a clicker goes like this (you will need a helper). Hold a treat in one hand and make both hands into fists. Offer both fists to your dog, and, when he nudges the correct hand, your helper clicks immediately and you open the hand holding the treat.

(Instead of using a clicker, you can also use your tongue to make a clicking sound and condition your dog to that instead.) In the case of deaf dogs, a brief flash from a torch can replace the 'click.'

Dogs love this type of training; try it and you, too, will end up shouting "Click, click, hooray!" like me!

shortly before this we rewarded him for something completely different. Experts have determined the exact time frame for association: the maximum amount of time that can elapse before we praise and reward is 30 seconds – so be quick!

Clicker conditioning

Timing the use of praise very precisely is made easier by using a clicker; you simply have to condition your dog to the clicker and the clicking sound becomes the same as praise for him. This happens more

Time to rest, finally

You must have an active dog, otherwise you would not be reading this book, probably! But can he also relax and be calm? Even when playtime's over, the internal rev counter of many dogs is still going nineteen to the dozen, and it can also be that a dog who has played lots of games, and had plenty of fun and challenges, suddenly starts demanding more and more activities. If he doesn't let up, what should you do? In my experience, there are three things that help in this situation: relaxation, dedicated places for taking a break, and taboo zones.

Massage using small, circular movements

The TTouch technique was developed by Linda Tellington-Jones, and incorporates small movements which have a big impact. They don't just allow a dog to quieten, but also improve his concentration and awareness of his body, and deepen the bond between dog and human.

A basic explanation of TTouch is that you massage your dog all over using small, circular movements, and always more than just one complete circle. Circle your fingertips all over the dog's body, with enough pressure to move the skin. As is typical of someone who is a writer, I learnt TTouch from books, though I think it is better to attend a TTouch training course.

Obviously, you can massage or stroke

your dog using other methods. I also found other excellent suggestions in two other books: *Dog Relax – relaxed dogs, relaxed owners* and *The Complete Dog Massage Manual* (both Hubble & Hattie), both of which contain excellent advice and information on different ways to be in touch with your dog.

Take a break!

'Time out' involves no toys and no touching; you simply send your dog to his basket or onto his blanket for a while. Dedicate a space for this somewhere in your living area, and if he moves away from here, immediately bring him back. Praise him when he stays lying down whilst you are getting on with other things – at first in the same room and then elsewhere in the house.

Your dog will quickly settle into this special space and feel quietly comfortable there.

No playing here!

No matter how much you play with your dog, and how many different games you play, always make sure you have a no-play zone somewhere in your house; for example, a specific room where you do not ever play. The most your dog can expect in this room is a chewy bone to entertain him. In my house, the no-play zone is, for example, the living room. Why? A dog who is easily motivated to play reacts to the smallest indication that there might be a possibility of a game. Indoors – and specifically in the living room – Jaden knows that he might just as well stay lying down; he's not going to get any kind of game, so he may as well get his statutory 16 hours of sleep and gather his strength for active walks involving at least one toy, two exuberant children and lots of new ideas that I just have to try out with him. And how about you? Want to come and play, too?

Take a break!

1-4 Birthe tells Sam to "take a break!" and sends him to his blanket for some time out. To help Sam relax, she strokes and massages him lightly, and scratches his favourite spot behind his ears.

Interestingly, a dog's ears are a key area in all types of massage. As Sabina Pilguj, author of Dog Relax, says: "Ear massage very quickly calms and relaxes ... in my experience, this can combat anxiety, and is also helpful in helping your dog cope with extreme stress. Ear massage has been a great help when my dogs have felt insecure, been excited or anxious."

A perfect conclusion to play and training sessions!

A break in play: check

√ Keep paying attention - observe and interpret canine (learning) behaviour

√ Use positive reinforcement to motivate your dog

√ Try and use clicker training for playing and training purposes

√ Massage and TTouch - these also work to relax a person!

√ Set up no-play zones in your house

√ Introduce a dedicated quiet zone to help your dog calm down after play or exercise

√ Enjoy your dog to the full!

Index of games

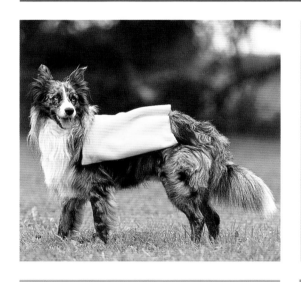

Further reading & information

Books

Blenski, Christiane
Dog speak: recognising and understanding behaviour
An uncomplicated, yet extremely informative guide to how we can understand our dogs properly. Dogs use their whole body to communicate – teeth, ears, eyes, fur, tail, body posture– and this volume explains the meaning behind this body language, whilst providing background information and practical tips. A highly entertaining book, and an invaluable reference for any dog lover.

Donaldson, Jean
Dogs are from Neptune
How humans and dogs get on successfully. Jean Donaldson shows us that dogs are different from us and how we can communicate with them. A liberating perspective that will change the way dogs and humans live together.

Pilguj, Sabina
Dog Relax – relaxed dogs, relaxed owners
Dogs and owners can relax through a combination of breathing and movement exercises, stretching and massage. This lovely book holds the secret to a different approach to living and working with your dog.

Birmelin, Immanuel
Know your dog – the guide to a beautiful relationship
Get to know your loyal friend from a different perspective through simple routines and games that you can have fun doing at home. Know your dog much better as the relationship between you becomes even deeper.

Pryor, Karen
Don't shoot the dog!
An American bestseller and a book that everyone should have. Use positive reinforcement to achieve incredible successes with the no-force, no-punishment method. Try it out!

Theby, Viviane
Smellorama! Nose games for dogs
Teach your faithful friend how to find those lost car keys, tell you if your food contains minute traces of nuts, or even how to locate a missing person: with these nose games, learning how is great fun for you both!

Tellington-Jones, Linda
The Tellington TTouch for dogs and puppies
More than massage, Linda Tellington-Jones' unique TTouch method comprises gentle strokes that reduce stress, anxiety or pain, and increase your dog's motivation and ability to learn. Very simple, and can be used whenever you like. For more vitality and a harmonious partnership with your dog.

Schops, Martina & Pick, Claudia
Dog cookies: healthy allergen-free treat recipes for your dog
You don't always have to buy treats – you can make them yourself. Some excellent, healthy recipes can be found in this book.

Internet
www.clickertraining.com (Karen Pryor's website)
www.flyballfever.co.uk
www.dogagility.org.uk
www.k9freestyle.co.uk
www.k9obedience.co.uk
www.caninetherapy.co.uk (dog massage)
www.blenski-dogs.com

More great Hubble & Hattie books!

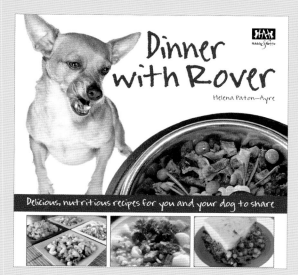

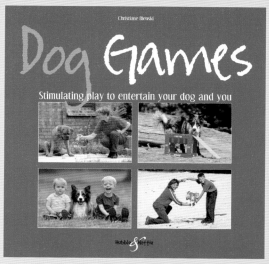

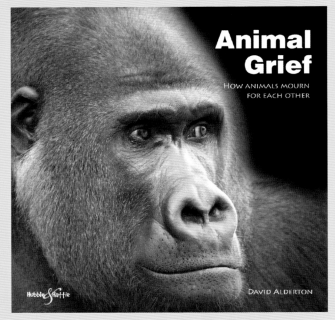

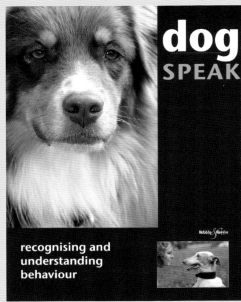

978-1-845842-88-8 £9.99*   978-1-845843-84-7 £9.99*   978-1-845843-85-4 £9.99*

www.hubbleandhattie.com

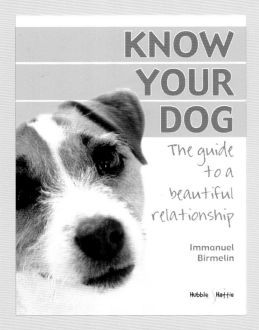

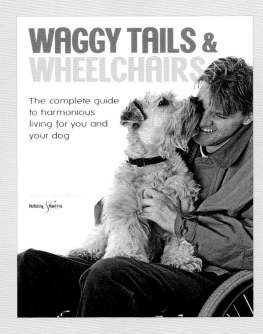

978-1-845840-72-3 £9.99*   978-1-845842-92-5 £12.99*   978- 1-845842-93-2 £9.99*

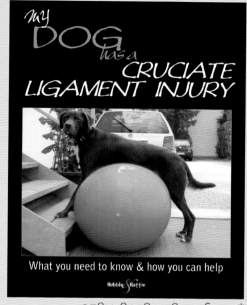

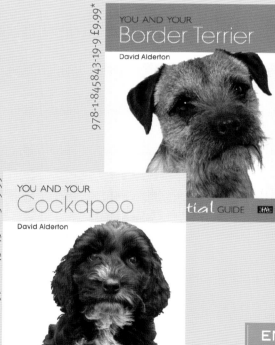

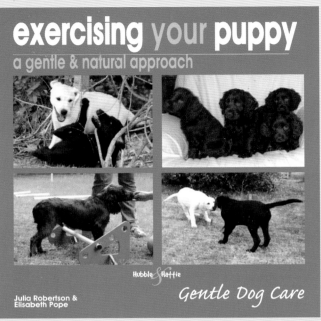
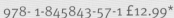
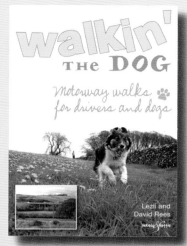

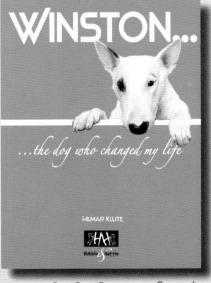